ISBN 978-1-5277-4183-6
PIBN 10886302

English
Français
Deutsche
Italiano
Español
Português

www.forgottenbooks.com

Mythology Photography **Fiction**
Fishing Christianity **Art** Cooking
Essays Buddhism Freemasonry
Medicine **Biology** Music **Ancient
Egypt** Evolution Carpentry Physics
Dance Geology **Mathematics** Fitness
Shakespeare **Folklore** Yoga Marketing
Confidence Immortality Biographies
Poetry **Psychology** Witchcraft
Electronics Chemistry History **Law**
Accounting **Philosophy** Anthropology
Alchemy Drama Quantum Mechanics
Atheism Sexual Health **Ancient History**
Entrepreneurship Languages Sport
Paleontology Needlework Islam
Metaphysics Investment Archaeology
Parenting Statistics Criminology
Motivational

Technical and Bibliographic Notes / Notes techniques

The Institute has attempted to obtain the best original copy available for filming. Features of this copy which may be bibliographically unique, which may alter any of the images in the reproduction, or which may significantly change the usual method of filming are checked below.

L'Institut a microfilm été possible de se plaire qui sont peut ographique, qui peu ou qui peuvent exig de normale de filma

☐ Coloured covers /
Couverture de couleur

☐ Covers damaged /
Couverture endommagée

☐ Covers restored and/or laminated /
Couverture restaurée et/ou pelliculée

☐ Cover title missing / Le titre de couverture manque

☑ Coloured maps / Cartes géographiques en couleur

☐ Coloured ink (i.e. other than blue or black) /
Encre de couleur (i.e. autre que bleue ou noire)

☐ Coloured plates and/or illustrations /
Planches et/ou illustrations en couleur

☐ Bound with other material /
Relié avec d'autres documents

☐ Only edition available /
Seule édition disponible

☐ Tight binding may cause shadows or distortion along interior margin / La reliure serrée peut causer de l'ombre ou de la distorsion le long de la marge intérieure.

☐ Blank leaves added during restorations may appear within the text. Whenever possible, these have been omitted from filming / Il se peut que certaines pages blanches ajoutées lors d'une restauration apparaissent dans le texte, mais, lorsque cela était possible, ces pages n'ont pas été filmées.

☐ Coloured page

☐ Pages damage

☐ Pages restore
Pages restaur

☑ Pages discolo
Pages décolor

☐ Pages detach

☑ Showthrough /

☑ Quality of print
Qualité inégal

☐ Includes suppl
Comprend du

☐ Pages wholly
tissues, etc., h
possible ima
partiellement o
pelure, etc., o
obtenir la meill

☐ Opposing pa
discolourations
possible image
colorations va
filmées deux f
possible.

Additional comments /

been reproduced thanks

y of Canada

e are the best quality
ondition and legibility
n keeping with the
tions.

paper covers are filmed
over and ending on
d or illustrated impres-
hen appropriate. All
ilmed beginning on the
r illustrated impres-
st page with a printed

n each microfiche
     (meaning "CON-
▽ (meaning "END").

may be filmed at
Those too large to be
posure are filmed
hand corner, left to
s many frames as
grams illustrate the

2   3

L'exemplaire filmé fut reproduit grâce à la
générosité de:

Bibliothèque nationale du Canada

Les images suivantes ont été reproduites avec le
plus grand soin, compte tenu de la condition et
de la netteté de l'exemplaire filmé, et en
conformité avec les conditions du contrat de
filmage.

Les exemplaires originaux dont la couverture en
papier est imprimée sont filmés en commençant
par le premier plat et en terminant soit par la
dernière page qui comporte une empreinte
d'impression ou d'illustration, soit par le second
plat, selon le cas. Tous les autres exemplaires
originaux sont filmés en commençant par la
première page qui comporte une empreinte
d'impression ou d'illustration et en terminant par
la dernière page qui comporte une telle
empreinte.

Un des symboles suivants apparaitra sur la
dernière image de chaque microfiche, selon le
cas: le symbole ⟶ signifie "A SUIVRE", le
symbole ▽ signifie "FIN".

Les cartes, planches, tableaux, etc., peuvent être
filmés à des taux de réduction différents.
Lorsque le document est trop grand pour être
reproduit en un seul cliché, il est filmé à partir
de l'angle supérieur gauche, de gauche à droite,
et de haut en bas, en prenant le nombre
d'images nécessaire. Les diagrammes suivants
illustrent la méthode.

1

MICROCOPY RESOLUTION TEST CHART

(ANSI and ISO TEST CHART No. 2)

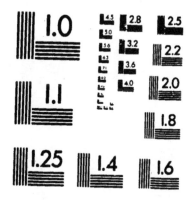

APPLIED IMAGE Inc

1653 East Main Street
Rochester, New York   14609   USA
(716) 482 - 0300 - Phone
(716) 288 - 5989 - Fax

CONCISE HISTORY

OF

ICELAND

TRANSLATED BY

JON G. PALMESON.

Of Ottawa, Ont., Canada,

From the original work in Icelandic.

WRITTEN BY

BOGI MELSTED

COPENHAGEN.

PREFACE BY THE AUTHOR.

Everybody is aware that the people of all civilized nations desire to have their children taught the history of their country and with this object in view we beg to introduce this little work, on the history of Iceland, which we trust will prove interesting to young and old and fill a long felt want; that of a concise history of our country.

We do not attempt, in this little work, to notice the names of all our nation's leaders or all the national events, but the names and incidents mentioned will no doubt interest our teachers and our scholars. It will enable these to learn, in a short time, and have a general insight to the names of our great men and note the principal events connected with our Icelandic history. The chief aim of this work is to impress upon you the primitive history of Iceland and therefrom trace the advance of civilization with its bearings on our nationality and peculiar characteristics, the finance of the country and condition of the people.

BOGI TH MELSTED,
Author.

Copenhagen, 1903, A.D.

INTRODUCTION.

—

Dear Reader:

I trust you will bear with me in this, my first, endeavor to give you an insight into the ancient history of Iceland and trust that the following chapters may interest not only yourself, but also others, who may desire to gain a knowledge of the progression of Iceland, from the earliest times to the present date.

As you are aware it is very difficult to place before you in an efficient and proper manner, an almost literal translation which can be easily understood, to thoroughly interest the reader. But I have in this work endeavored to translate the original into readable English.

sincerely hope that this, my maiden effort, may be the means of causing the outside world to become more acquainted not only with our history, manners and customs from early times But prove to the world at large that Iceland has a history peculiarly her own.

My readers will notice by reference to the map I have caused to be inserted in the work, the divisions into which the land was divided in ancient times and will find it a guide to the better understanding of the topography of the Island.

I have also inserted several portraits of eminent men mentioned.

I must thank MR. A. W. DICKSON for his able assistance in helping me to put this work in appropriate form, but at the same time should there be found any mistakes, he is not responsible for them.

With these few remarks I now leave the work for your perusal, and hope it will be of interest to you, and that you will by my feeble effort gain a better knowledge of the history of a comparatively unknown country.

THE TRANSLATOR.

THE
DISCOVERY OF ICELAND

—o—

CELAND is an island situated on the North Atlantic, and is found between the paral' '. 63 deg. 24 min. and 66 deg. 33 min. North Latitude and the Meridians 15 deg. 45 min. and 26 deg. 50 min. West Longitude.

The nearest countries are, Norway to the East and Ireland and some of the Northern Isles of Scotland to the South.

The Vikings of Norway, those adventurou, mariners of olden times, the greatest sailors of that period, were the first to discover Iceland. One of these named Naddodd was the first to set foot in our country, this was in the year 861, A.D. As soon as winter came on, he prepared to return to his native land. He noticed the mountain peaks were covered with snow and the climate was exceed-. ingly cold and he appropriately called this newly discovered country Snowland.

In the year 865, A.O., another of the Vikings, by the name of Gardar, visited the Island and after having navigated his ship around the Island, called it after himself, Gardar's Island.

In the year 867, A.D., a third adventurer, by the name of Floki, on arriving, disembarked his men and concluded to settle on the Island, taking ashore what live stock they had with them. The landing was made in the broad bay, on the west side of the Island. However, as fishing was extremely good, they neglected to make any provision for winter provender for their live stock, so that, in consequence of their not cutting any hay during the summer, all of their live stock died that winter. While Floki was exploring round the coast, he noticed quantities of Polar Ice on the northern shores, so he called the country Iceland, and by that name it has ever since been known.   Floki resided there two winters only and returned to Norway in the year 869, A.O.

Colonizing of Iceland.

In the year 873, A.D., two wealthy Vikings, by the names of Ingolf and Hjorleif, determined on exploring the Island, to find out whether it was a desirable place to settle in or not, and having satis-fied themselves on the desirability of settling there, returned to Norway, and in 874, A.D., set sail in two large trading ships, taking with them their wives, slaves and all necessary provisions and articles for founding their new homes and also a number of horses, cattle and sheep.

Hjorleif landed on the east side of the Island and named the spot Cape Hjorleif.   Here he erected a dwelling and out-buildings, and resided during the following winter.

Hjorleif was a Viking, and having captured ten men in Ireland before he came out, made slaves of them and set them to plow up a piece of land, in which he desired to sow some rye which he had brought over with him.   But the slaves rebelled and killed Hjorleif and all his men, but spared the women, whom they took with them to some islands in the southeast. These are called Westman Islands today, after the name of the country the slaves came from.

Ingolf, having separated from his friend on sighting Iceland, caused his high seat posts to be brought to him and, forthwith, threw them overboard, and turning to his people said: We will settle where the gods will to leave them.

In the meantime he landed on the east side of the Island, but considerably farther north of where his friend Hjorlief had, at a point he called Cape Ingolf, by which name it is known today. Here he stayed through the winter. The following spring he sent out his men along the coast to look for the high seat posts and they came as far south as Cape Hjorleif.

Here they found the massacred bodies of Hjorleif and his men.
So they returned to Ingolf and informed him of what they had seen.
When he had heard their story, he at once set out and on arrival
at Cape Hjorleif, he buried his friend and on discovering the where-
abouts of his friend's murderers he killed them and rescued the women.

That winter he stayed at Cape Hjorlief and started again to try
to find his high seat posts.   Residing the following winter at Mount
Ingolf, the next spring he was successful in his quest and found his
high seat posts washed ashore near Reykjavik, which place he made
his headquarters and residence.   He being the first actual settler
is naturally honored and revered by all Icelanders, and on the
ground he occupied is now situated the Capital of Iceland, a noble
monument of a grateful nation's memory of her first settler.

Harold Halfdanson (The Fair-haired.)
The Greatest of the Early Norman Kings.

For a great many years before ever Iceland was discovered,
Norway was divided up into many small kingdoms, the rulers of
which were continually fighting against each other.   About the
time of the settlement in Iceland the most powerful of these was
Harold Halfdanson, who succeeded in conquering all the other
kings and killed all their relatives to serve his own ends.   He was
a tyranical ruler and oppressed the farmers by exacting heavy taxes
and finally took possession of all the country and made the people
pay him rent for the land, a precedent never before established in
the country and therefore objectionable to the leading men of Norway.   So rather than submit, they emigrated to Iceland, Scotland
and Ireland.   Thus Iceland was largely settled by these men.

The First Colonists of Iceland.

The first homesteaders in Iceland took up a large piece of land,
on which they erected large buildings for their dwellings and cultivated what is called a Homefield round about their homes, which

they thoroughly cultivated and which their descendants still hold and till the soil of as their ancestors did, but of course with much improved methods at the present time.

In 60 years after this Iceland was about as thickly settled as it is today, the original settlers dividing their property with these who came at a later date, so that every one was possessed of a share of the land which naturally caused a good feeling between them.

The Book of Colonization.

This work is the oldest ever written in Iceland and was compiled from A.D. 1200 to A.D. 1300. It is the progenitor of the history of the nation. It contains not only the names of the first 400 settlers, that is the head men, but describes acurately where they settled it, also gives a brief account of their lineage and a biography.

The greater number of these settlers were, either descendants of the old Norman kings, or chiefs of clans, in Denmark, Scotland or Ireland, men who have been Vikings, who owned and sailed their own vessels and carried cargoes of settlers' effects and live stock.

Iceland of a Thousand Years Ago.

A large portion of the land was covered with trees, but of stunted growth and small size, and in the low lands there were hay meadows, so that the settlers found ample grazing for their stock, which gave them great encouragement. But as they became more numerous they used to turn it out in these woods in the winter time, and as there was no other feed for the stock they destroyed the bark and the trees naturally soon died. Fishing was to be had in abundance, not only in the lakes and rivers, but also in the sea, whales being plentiful. Birds of all kinds were to be had in great numbers also.

So many people emigrated from Norway to Iceland that King Harold became very much dissatisfied, as he had no control over

Iceland, it being at that time an independent colony, so he sent a man, by the name of Uni Gardarson, on a voyage to Iceland with the object of annexing the country and bringing it under his rule. Harold promised Uni the Earldom of Iceland in recognition of his services. Having made his preparations and equipped his ships with all necessaries for the voyage, in due time arrived. In stating the object of his visit and showing the king of Norway's commission to the people, they refused to either let him have provisions, or allow him the use of their horses to make excursions into the country. He was an exceedingly wicked man and the natives rose up and slew him. This was the first and only attempt that King Harold ever made to annex Iceland to the Kingdom of Norway.

The Religion, Temples and Priests.

Most of the Icelanders, at this time, were heathen, as also were the Norsemen and with the exception of a few who had emigrated from Ireland, they worshiped the Deities. Odin, who was thought to be the Chief of the Gods, and Thor, the god of Thunder and of Battle, and was considered the strongest god. Many of the leaders or chief men built temples of worship, which were made of ordinary timber, but the interiors were grandly finished, as they thought the gods would be more easily propitiated if they had comfortable dwellings, where the worshippers assembled. The owner of a temple was called a priest and his neighbors, many of whom could not afford to build a temple for themselves and relations, used to go to these priests' temples, to worship the gods and paid a tithe or tax, called 'Temple Tax' to the priest who was considered a chief or leader in his community and had immense powers and influence, but in later years when the Constitution was established by accord of the people and approved, the number and power of these temple-masters was curtailed.

The First Althing of Iceland.

Up to this time the people of Iceland had no statutory laws or courts of justice to make proper laws for their government or unite the people.   All they had was a national language.

However, Thorstein Ingolfson, who resided in Reykjavik, got the people together and called an assembly of people of the south-quarter to a 'Kjalnesthing' or legislative assembly and caused to be appointed juries, not only to try the criminal cases, but also to settle disputes and disagreements between settlers.   This was the first legislative assembly ever in Iceland.

A certain man by the name of Ulfljot, went over to Norway to learn what he could of 'Gulathings law' called at that time 'Breast law.'   He remained and studied in Norway for three years, when he returned to Iceland thoroughly posted and learned in the law. This 'Breast law,' as it was called, became the popular law of the Icelanders and was by them called 'Norwegian law.'   It had been in force in Norway for many years and the people of Iceland were somewhat acquainted with it, also with Norwegian rule generally. So Ulfljot educated many of the young men in the law and they became lawyers.

The Althing Organized

As soon as a suitable spot could be found, the people came to it and held thereon what was called 'Althing' or Congress, and the place named "Congress lawn' or 'Thingvall' at that time they had no building to meet in but all the population were called together to discuss and hear the Norwegian law.   And it was adapted as the law for the future of Icelandic government.   A republic was established by these means in the year 930, and they protected their autonomy for more than three centuries or up to 1264.

Icelandic Republic.

The first period of our history after the full settlement of the country was when the Republic was organized, which was during the years 930-1030, was called the Historical Century on account of the number of great events which happened during this period.

The prominent leaders, the many battles which they fought, the doubty deeds done by those strong but wicked heroes, whose strength and hardihood make us of the present day wonder at. Their intelligence, progression and prophetic spirit were marvellous and how it was that they were able to foretell future events so many years ahead is beyond our power to realize. We will here give a short epitome of some of them in this little history.

Egill Skallagrimson's Biography and History of His Relatives.

He was a great leader and warrior. His residence was at Borg, in the south part of the country, at the same place in which his father had settled. Egill was an extremely large man and is thought to have been the strongest man Iceland ever knew, a brave man and a great Viking.

Eirik Haroldson, who was king of Norway at this time, hated Egill. Egill was always fighting with his friends and in one of the battles he killed his own son, Rognvald. He was an intelligent, active and energetic man and well educated, he has been and is still considered the first and best poet of the Historical Century.

The largest and best story, written in these early times, is the biography of Njal and his sons, who resided at Bergthorshvoli. That of Gunnar, who lived at Hlidarenda, is also interesting. He was a very large man, very strong, a great athlete and a thorough master in the art of war. He went over to Norway, where he stayed for many years and became a Viking. He became famous amongst the fighters and had a great name on his return to Iceland. He amassed considerable wealth and married a widow, whose name was Hallgerd. She was a very handsome woman but wicked, having had two husbands, both of whom she caused to be murdered. She caused Gunnar an immense amount of trouble and he had many fights on her account and was ordered into exile for the term of three years by the 'Court Board' and refused to be reconciled to them. He was finally killed by his enemies.

He was a man of fine physique, great ability, was constant and true to his friends and much loved and regretted by his country men.

Njal was a peace loving man and was the greatest lawyer of his age and known all over Iceland for his wisdom, peaceful ways, and mediatory methods in settling feuds or trouble amongst the people. He was one of the prime movers in organizing laws and regulations regarding the peace and prosperity of the country and its people. He was a great friend of Gunnar and on one occasion said to him: "If you do not refuse to be reconciled to the 'Court Board' you will be victorious," but Gunnar would rather die than leave the place he was born in.

Njals sons, more especially one by name of Skarphjedin, were wicked. Presumably this could be accounted for on account of the Viking blood flowing in their veins.

Njal had a foster son, called Hoskuld. He became a leader of a constituence near his home, and another leader not far from him was called Mord. He was a very bad man and envied Hoskuld's success and honest ways. So he enveigled himself into the good graces of Njal's sons and they became great friend. He worked on their feelings to such an extent that by slandering Hoskuld, he induced them to murder their foster brother, whom the people knew to be an innocent man. So the relatives and friends of Hoskuld got together at the home of the Njals, set fire to the house and burned them and their father and mother. They offered to spare the father and mother, but they refused and said they would rather die than live, after this disgraceful act of their sons.

The Althing or Congress.

The Althing was called to meet on Thingvall, (or Congress lawn), every year in the latter end of June and this was made a law. It was imperitive for the pronouncing lawyer or head leader and the others to be there at the appointed time and anyone owning real estate, was forced to either meet on the Thingvall or pay a fine to their leaders. This law was also put in the statutes.

All the national laws were made and fixed by the Althing and all cases of breach of laws or disputes were settled by the Judicial Court, the lawyers pleading as at the present day for either plaintiff or defendant.

The legislators or law makers of the old Icelandic commonwealth laws, consisted of a pronouncing lawyer, the leaders and two men with each leader. The pronouncing lawyer or declarator was president of the Judicial Court and it was his duty to read and interpret the law and thoroughly explain it to the Althing, or people assembled. The particular place from which the laws were given out was called the 'Logberg.'

As soon as the Althing became recognized as the governing body, the Judicial Court was organized. In the year 965 the whole land was divided into four quarters, namely, south quarter, west quarter, north quarter, east quarter, and at a later date the Judicial Court was also divided in like manner, one court for each quarter. THE JURY. If a jury, which consisted of 12 men, were unable to agree on a subject, the case was dismissed and thus many cases were closed without either party getting satisfaction. In the first years of the eleventh century, that is about the year 1004, a High Court was organized; this consisted of a grand jury of 48 men, whose business it was to settle every case brought before them.

Althing was considered a great place to spend a pleasant time and see and hear instructive and entertaining amusements, which made it very interesting to young or old assembled, both men and women, the leaders and farmers to tend to their duties every day. The young people took a great interest in all the proceedings and had great times playing games and hearing stories of other lands, as story-tellers were men of talent and were clever in reciting folk lore of other countries.

The Quarter Things.

When the Althing was thoroughly organized and had become a national affair, the four quarters, east, north, west and south of

Iceland were sub-divided into counties, each county consisting of one third of the quarter, with the exception of the northern quarter which was divided into four counties, the northern quarter as it was called, having much larger area than the others. Each of the counties sent representatives to the Althing, each county sending 3 representatives, but the northern sent 12. This made a sum total of 40 representatives or legislators, one being elected the pronouncing lawyer or head of the legislature. These men met in the month of May and the convocation was called quarter-thing. They appointed the jury who looked into and passed on all question of law that were not carried up to the Althing.

After the session of Althing was closed, the quarter master summoned the people of the 'quarter-thing' to meet again, at which meeting he informed the people of all new laws adopted by Althing and explained their meaning and use. These quarter masters, however, had no judicial power, but acted as informants or teachers, as it were, for the members of the quarter-thing.

Greenland and Vineland Discovered.

During the colonization century, of which we have already spoken, a certain man, whose name we cannot recall, was caught in a severe storm off the west coast of Iceland and his vessel was driven before the wind so far west that he sighted land hitherto unknown and unheard of by the people of Iceland. But it was but a short time before the news of his discovery became general and his report was believed to be true, that more land existed in the Western Ocean, as the Northern Atlantic was then called. About this time a wicked Viking, whose name was Eirik Thorvaldson living in the west, near Broad Bay, was convicted for criminal offences and sentenced to 3 years' exile. He set sail in a western direction and discovered a large area of mainland, where, having disembarked, he resided for the period of his sentence. On returning to Iceland he spoke in such praise of this new country, which he called Greenland, that he induced many Icelanders to emigrate, telling them that it was a good country. On settling there, which was about the year 986, they were content to follow the laws and rules that were already in use in their native land.

About the year 1000, one Leif, a son of Eirik, discovered land still further west, and on account of the quantity of vineberries growing there, he called it Vineland.

Many people wished to settle on this new land, but as it was peopled with hostile Indians, they concluded to return to Greenland. This Vineland was on the eastern shores of North America.

Iceland Christianized.

When Iceland was settled Ireland, Scotland and England were already Christianized, but the northern portion of Europe still embraced the heathen religion. But as soon as Denmark began to embrace Christianity, it was but a short time before it spread into Iceland.

In 981 the first two Christian missionaries landed in Iceland, who were named Thorvald Kodranson and Frederik. The former was an Icelander of good family, and the latter was a Romish bishop.

Thorvald was a well educated and extremely good man and desirous to introduce Christianity into his native land and having found that the Christian religion was so far superior to heathen doctrine, he persuaded the bishop, Frederik, who was a German, to accompany him to Iceland and try to induce his relatives and country men to become converts, to which the bishop after considering the matter consented.

During the first winter of their sojourn in Iceland they resided with Thorvald's father, who, with all his people, became Christians. Thorvald and his friend, the bishop, remained for several winters in the north quarter and a few of the people became Christians. In June they went to Althing, speaking of and instructing in the Christian religion, aiming at introducing Christianity all over the land. But this so excited the people that for fear of assassination they fled from the country.

In the year 995 Olaf Triggvason became king of Norway. He was a zealous man and a good Christian, and he was anxious that all Norwegians and all countries where any of them had settled and were in habited by the descendants of the ancient Norman race (Scandinavians) should become Christianized So he hired one, whose name was Stefnir, an Icelander, to go to his country and endeavor to Christianize the people, viz., the ancient Norwegians, who were the first settlers of Iceland, but Stefnir met with so much opposition that he was only too glad to return to Norway.

King Olaf was not disheartened, but sent another missionary, a priest, called Thangbrand. He stayed for two years and amongst others he baptized several of the leaders, among whom were Hjalte Skeggjason, Hall Thordarson and Gissur. The priest was a wicked man and killed several of his enemies and then returned to Norway, where he had an interview with the king and excused his failure by telling him that the heathen religion was so deeply rooted in Iceland that it was almost impossible to ever hope to see it Christianized. The king on hearing this, flew into a rage, he being a very quick tempered man and threated to kill any Icelander who was living at that time in Norway.

Hjalte and Gissur, who left Iceland during the same summer as Thangbrand, hurriedly called all their countrymen together to look into the matter and try to devise some means of allaying the king's anger and the people unanimously elected Hjalte and Gissur delegates to make a compromise. Having arrived in Norway they sought out the king and had an audience with him and after pleading their case the king made an agreement with them to spare all the Icelanders in Norway on condition that they became Christians. This was successful, as they were easily persuaded by the bishops. Hjalte and Gissur also agreed to sail the following summer for Iceland with the object of converting the Icelanders to Christianity. When the time came they set sail, accompanied by a priest, by the name of Thormod. They landed about the time of the sitting of Althing, and the priest delivered a powerful address to all the

Christians who were there assembled. After he finished Hjalte made known the king's wishes and spoke at great length on the subject. This so affected the heathen leaders that they declared that they would have no more to do with the Christian ment, but would have a pronouncing lawyer of their own and accordingly appointed a man by the name of Thorgeir. He had been a leader before and although a heathen, was a just, upright, honest and highly intelligent man of good morals and was always listened to with great respect by the people when he addressed them. He however cooperated with Hall, who was the Christian leader, and finally Thorgeir was accepted as president for both parties. For 24 hours before addressing the Althing, he absented himself and shut himself up in his tent covered with ropes and fasted and refused to speak to any one. At the end of this time he rose and walked to Logberg and having taken his accustomed place, he sent out word to the people and the result was the greatest convention ever held in Iceland. He then delivered the speech, which has made him famous, commencing by saying that, 'If the law is divided then peace will be no more.' He impressed upon the people the terrible state the country would be in if the legislative body were divided and there was no oneness in religion and said we must have one statute and one religion. This speech so wrought the people up that they all sided with him and the whole national party promised to accept and obey the proposed statute, one passage of which read as follows: 'Every man, woman and child, throughout the length and breadth of the land, who has not already been, shall be baptized and become Christians,' he disregarded some of their heathen propensities, as these disappeared without trouble in the year 1000.

King Olaf Haraldson's Attempt to Conquer Iceland.

Up to this time Iceland was an independent nation, the inhabitants making their living by farming and raising stock and fishing, but had commercial intercourse with Norway and some othe tries and they did a great deal of trading among themsel ch

made them very successful and prosperous as a nation. The Icelanders were greatly esteemed and highly honored by all the Norwegian rulers who thought so much of Iceland that they tried to
annex the country on several occasions.

Olaf Haroldson was made king of Norway in the year 1015.
He was an able statesman and a good king and ruled with justice.
He was a great supporter of the Christian religion and tried his
best to Christianize all colonies that were inhabited by Norwegians
or settled by them, Iceland being among the number. He induced
a man, Skapta Thoroduson, at that time president of the Icelandic
Republic, as it was then called, to bring before the Althing at the
Court of Arbitration, a law to abolish the heathen custom habit,
which was detrimental to the country, and this he succeeded in ac-
complishing.

With the introduction of Christianity peace and prosperity
reigned in the little Republic. But King Olaf with all his good
qualities, was of a domineering and ambitious temperment, and he
desired very much to annex Iceland and consequently endangered
the liberty of the people. The Icelanders were in the habit of trading with Norway every year, to which place they went with their
ships laden and returned with necessaries from Norway and other
places. He tried to ingratiate himself with these leaders and their
sons.

Owing to the climate they went to Norway in the summer and
remained there over the winter and returned home the following
spring, remaining at home during the next winter and the following
spring taking another commercial trip to Norway.

Owing to this ancient commercial rule, the king was able to
speak with all the wealthy leaders of Iceland and their sons, and
he tried to ingratiate himself into their good graces .

Nearly all the young men were of highly respectable families
and they took these trips for the benefit of their education.

In the year 1024, King Olaf induced a man named Thordur
Nefjolfson, an Icelander, to go to Iceland, and gave him a commis

sion to present to the Althing, asking the people to become his subjects and give over to him an island at that time uninhabited called
'Grims Island.' Some of the leaders were willing to submit, so
they called a meeting and discussed the matter in full. One man,
Einar by name, made a very eloquent speech there. He said:
'We must take great pains in considering this matter, so vital to
our nation, and must on no account do anything that will interfere
with our national prerogative; we must look after our own interest,
but above all, we must firmly refuse to put ourselves under subjec-
tion to the King of Norway. Should we do so, we would be bur-
dened with taxes and expenses incurred, at the same time depriving
ourselves of our social liberty and that of our descendants for ever.'
Referring to the island, he said: 'Should we give the king Grims
Island, it would place him in a position that would enable him to
send there an army of occupation which would be a great menace
to us and as fish and fowl are there in good quantities, he could
feed them at little expense and we would also have to face the fact
that his war vessels, being almost at our doors would continually
harass us and we could not possibly escape becoming subjects of the
Norwegian kingdom, our land annexed, our liberty lost, our legal
rights trampled on and made subservient to kingly rule for ever.'

When Einar had finished his speech, the whole national body
concurred with him, and so Olaf found it impossible to annex Iceland.

The Peace Century 1030-1118.
Peace, Prosperity and Civilization.

Under heathen rule the country was always in feuds or at war,
the prestige of the ancient Vikings being upheld by this means.
But on the introduction of Christianity there was more sociability
amongst the inhabitants, and not only that, but peace brought content and a greater amount of humane laws and regulations which
the people found very difficult to follow for some time. In the
year 1030 the national feuds and the inherent hostility was almost
abolished and peace and prosperity reigned for nearly a century and

is called)y the historians of otr cotntry The Peace Century. When Christianity was an accepted fact, the intercotrse between heathen and Christian in all religious matters were less strained and the constitution of the cotntry was greatly improved)y the forming of the grand jtry and more eqtality between leaders, their power)eing weakencd and more limited by the discontinuance of the mythological orgies. They erected churches instead of temples, and several of the men received stfficient edtcation as to warrant them becoming priests.

Bishop Isleif.

In the early Christian times, all the bishops sent from Rome to Iceland were foreigners and did all they cotld to)ring the people to the knowledge of Christian doctrine, and were thorotghly convinced of the necessity and the great responsi)ility under which they were placed, so they importtned one of their country)en, whose name was Isleif, a good man and thcroughly edtcated priest, to)e their bishop. He had received a good collegiate edtcation in Germany (and)eing an ertdite)an was best fitted for the plaçe.)

The Pope sancfioned their reqtest. He was called to Rome to interview his holiness who was the head of all Christendom and stccessor of St. Peter. The Pope was sc pleased with Isleif that he ordered the Bishop of Brimum, who was arch)ishop for the whole of Northern Etrope, to ordain Isleif as Bishop of Iceland. This occurred on Whitsunday, 1056. Isleif then went to Iceland and resided at Skalholt. He did his)est to improve the)orals of the people and induce them to beco)e Christians and also appointed a great many priests who did)tch to pro)ote the catse.

After the death of Isleif, his son, Gissur, took his place as his father's representative at the Althing)y reqtest of the people, and in accepting the trust, stipulated that the leaders shctld)e subservient to his direction and will in all matters pertaining to chtrch affairs.

Gissur was also a collegiate of a German University, and every one prophesied that he would become a great leader, so having gone to Rome he was ordained.

The Pope of Rome at that time was Gregory the Seventh, (called Gregory the great) who ruled the church with a strong hand, and in all he did showed immense energy and at the same time extreme intelligence.

He had complete command of the church, its bishops and priests, in fact, his word was law. It is well understood that he ordered Gissur to promulgate the Christian doctrine in Iceland and also to extend the power of the church. Gissur therefore made great efforts to obey the Pope, and succeeded in having erected the Cathedral at Skalholt, for which object he gave all his real estate and wealth, not only that at Skalholt, but what he had elsewhere. He also was the means of establishing by law the fact that the seat of Roman Catholicism should be forever situate at Skalholt and also that all real estate and personal property should be assessed and the amount of tax thus collected paid to the maintenance of the churches and priests and in part to the guardians of the poor, which naturally enriched the churches. After the first census was taken, Iceland was found to contain 4560 real estate owners. Bishop Gissur was a great administrator both in church matters and state affairs and ruled as bishop and king as long as he lived. He caused the nation to become peaceful and in many cases was the mediator between warring factions and settled many disputes which had arisen between the leaders. He died respected, honored and mourned for his honesty, straighforwardness, piety and generosity by the nation in the year 1118.

Jon, Bishop at Holum.

About the middle of the eleventh century the bishop, for the north quarter of Iceland, was an alien. He was a very pious and energetic man. At that time the work of a bishop was extremely ardious as he had a large territory to oversee and had to be continually travelling, consecrating churches and other buildings used for divine worship, confirming and communicating the people, and looking after the welfare of the churches and parishes.

After Skalholt had been established as the ruling see, the people of the north quarter sent a complaint to the bishop at Skalhott, stating that owing to the great distance they had to travel, they were put to not only a great expense but loss of time. So they begged Bishop Gissur to appoint or form another see in the north quarter, as they contended that it would be for the furtherment of Christianity. So having called all the leaders together in consultation it was decided to create a new see in the north quarter and at the people's request Jon Ogmundson, a very clever priest and sincere man, was ordained as bishop of the north of Iceland. The Pope had appointed an archbishop at Lundi for the northern see, but Jan Ogmundson sailed to Denmark, where he was ordained, returned to Iceland and went to Holt, a place donated by one of the priests for the bishop's residence. Through the energy of Jon Ogmundson he was successful in erecting a Cathedral there and founding a school for teaching and writing latin songs for which purpose he brought over several foreign professors. He took great pains to make the school as perfect as possible and beneficial to the scholars, he being the principal of it ruled it with a generous but firm hand.

Bishop Jon was a peacable and God-fearing man, devoted to the church, a great advocate of civil reforms and ardent preacher, and noted for his humility and generosity. His death took place in the year 1121.

1118-1200 Called the Writing Century.

The first written law in Iceland was what was called 'Fighting path.' This was written during the winter of 1117 and 1118 and had reference to war feids and other hostile matters which had or were occurring in the country; it was read and approved by Althing in 1118. The author of the work was Halflida Nasson and it was called the 'Haflida Code.' The writing of this work may be said to be the beginning of the written literature of Iceland, as other works or histories were written about this time or at least during the 12th century. Later on we shall hear of the word 'Writing Century.'

Rev. Ari Thorgilson.

The first and most notable author of Iceland was Ari Thorgilson, who was an extremely well educated man and well versed in the history of Iceland. He bought and gathered from all the people he could any information concerning the colony, its origin, manners and inhabitants from the earliest times. He wrote two books and called them 'Icelanders' Books.' He was 60 years old when he commenced to write them. The ruling bishops at that time were Thorlak and Ketill and it was by their command that the works were written. The first book contained a short epitome of the history of early Iceland and an account of the kings of Norway; the second, a brief history of Iceland and her inhabitants, manners and customs. Up to the year 1120 this was a small work, but contains a fund of information regarding the settlement of the land and the most prominent events in our history, the dates of each event being mentioned, makes it a valuable historical work and entitles Ari Thorgilson to the title of the first Icelandic historian. He lived until the year 1148 and died at the ripe old age of 80.

The Advance of Christian Religion and Erection of Monasteries.

Shortly after the death of Gissur the land was stricken and crops failed, causing a great famine to spread over the country and many of the inhabitants died from sheer starvation. The leaders became fractious and unruly, but Bishops Thorlak and Ketill became mediators between the parties and in a short time peace was restored and continued for the space of 50 years. The advance of civilization was greatly aided by the work of these two bishops. They also introduced a written ordinance called 'The Ancient Christians

Rights' which is still extant.   In the year 1133, through the energy of Bishop Ketill of Holum, a monastery was built at Thingey-
reum and dedicated, and at the latter part of the 12th century other
monasteries were built for the accommodation of the monks, one of
which at Flatey, was moved at a later date to Helgafell, also a nun-
nery was established at Kirkjuby.

Dissatisfaction—Jon Loptson and Bishop Thorlak.

During the latter part of the 12th century there was a great
deal of dissatisfaction between the leaders and many had resort to
arms.   The dissention started in the west quarter, when a man
named Sturla Thordarson became a prominent factor and in the
north quarter one of the leaders attacked and burned in his own
house another of the leaders.   This was in 1197.

The bishops, however, became the mediators, and one leader,
by the name of Jon Loptson, in conjunction with the bishops, succeeded in restoring peace.

About this time some of the leaders became very wicked and
loose in their morals, which caused great demoralization among the
lower classes.   Word of this came to the ears of the archbishop,
who resided at that time in Norway and he accordingly wrote some
letters to the bishops of Iceland, but could not succeed in doing much
good.   Iceland at that time was not entirely under the archbishop's
control, owing to the fact that they lived so far away and consequently were but little acquainted with the situation.   They resided at that time at   Brimum or Lundi.   The archbishop of Iceland was not a resident of Norway until the year 1152.

Commercial intercourse between Iceland and Norway gave him
an opportunity to become acquainted with the affairs and conditions
of church and state in Norway and Iceland.

In the year 1178 Thorlak Thorhallason was ordained by the archbishop, as bishop of Skalholt and he was commanded to take all the
churches and property belonging to them from the farmers in his

diocese. But as the farmers had built the churches and donated real estate and given personal property there to them, they considered that being part and parcel of their own property, they had a right to rule it for their own benefit, as well as the church's. The following summer at Althing Bishop Thorlak started to fulfil his commission, telling the people that he was ordered so to do by the archbishop and that the archbishop's word was law. But Jon Loptson, who was the head man, replied that they could not be subservient to any foreigner, nor had he any right to deprive them of their property. Seeing the temperament of the people on the subject, the bishop was deterred from trying to enforce his orders, as he saw it would cause great dissatisfaction and open hostility to the church.

Bishop Thorlak was a generous and just man, a moral philosopher and a reformer. He did his best to thoroughly civilize the people but failed in the attempt.

The moral law caused great dissatisfaction amongst the people, as it prevented 5th cousins from marrying.

Relative to the Education of Our Country.

During the latter part of the 12th and beginning of the 13th centuries the priests and monks wrote much of the history of Iceland and also about remarkable events that happened in early times. These facts had been handed down by word of mouth from generation to generation. These stories were much revered by the people and were greatly esteemed. Amongst the works written at that period were, not only, The beginning of the Icelandic history, the history of the Norwegian kings, but an account of the discovery of Greenland and of North America.

During 10th and 11th centuries there were a great many bards or poets in Iceland, who made trips to Norway and other foreign countries and they were received by the kings and leaders with whom they lived and for whom they wrote verses, many of which were greatly admired at that time and for which they were highly honored and rewarded.

There is one book of verses called Edda, and it is a large work on heathen mythology and has been used as a basis for Icelandic metre.

The heathens believed in many gods and this work explains what the ancients thought about them, of the wonderful deeds done by their heroes, informs us of the greatness of their philosophers and explains the various myths in connection with the lives of these gods. The principal deity was called Odin, who was considered a great philosopher and hero, and was supposed to be the father of the ancient kings of Northern Europe. The latter portion of the book is devoted to biographical data in verses, concerning the heroes of ancient times and they are highly praised for their valorious deeds.

It is thought that this ancient work is synonymous with the mythology of Greece as it follows the same lines and is very much admired as a fine art collection of ancient verses.

The Period From 1200 to 1264.

In the year 1200, the leaders of Iceland were surprised to find two great errors in the constitution, which had escaped notice during the proceeding centuries and nothing had been done to improve the constitutional law.

The first mistake they discovered was a passage, stating that any one leader could annex to himself another constituency, either by inheritance or purchase from another leader. So he was thus enabled to rule over and represent as many constituencies as he could either conquer or obtain, as at that time there was nothing in the constitution to prevent it. In the latter part of the 12th century some of the predominent leaders annexed many of the constituencies which made them haughty and upset the 'Equal Rights' which had saved the nation from internal wars.

The second error made in drawing up the constitution was, that no one was empowered by law to safeguard the rights of the people or to hold the leaders in check and force obedience to the law from them.

During the Historical Century, about which you have already heard, no leader was able to put into the field more than from 60 to 100 fighting men, but in the early part of the 13th century, (owing to the fact that some of the leaders by annexation ruled over a whole quarter of the land and could purchase the right to summon men to fight their battles), they could put into the field from 600 to 1000 men. They fought fierce and bloody battles with one another. The chief and strongest leaders were descendants of four highly respectable families, viz.: The Oddverjar and Haukdyl in the south quarter; Sturlung in the west, and Asbyrnings in the north.

Trouble Between the People and Clergy—Foreign Political Opinion is Mooted in the Island.

Hostilities began in earnest when Bishop Gudmund Arason demanded the right from the judicial court to govern the clergy himself. But this was refused and the people demanded that the clergy should be subservient to the constitutional laws, just the same as they were in the early days, when the island was Christianized. The bishop was allowed a seat in the legislative assembly with the same rights as the other leaders had. And there he discussed the laws for the government of churches, clergy and people and the priests had to obey the law and were under the same judicial jurisdiction as the people. With this exception, that in matters relating to clerical or church work, the bishop could settle them out of court.

The archbishop commanded Bishop Gudmund to endeavor to have the ordinance changed, but the Althing refused to make any alterations in the constitutional statutes.

Bishop Gudmund was a man of strong constitution and iron will, but as the leaders consisted of wealthy and unscrupulous men, there was considerable dissension between them and the bishop, and it took a long time and hard work on the part of the archbishop to become a mediator between them. But after a time some of the leaders were induced to refer to him for judgment and, it was by this means that the archbishop obtained a greater hold in the island and consequently more power. In the years 1217-19, a man who resided at Odda, whose name was Jonson, had a disagreement with some Norwegian merchants and Earl Skule, who was a ruler of Norway, at that time, knowing for a fact that the merchants had been honestly dealt with and unreasonably treated by the Icelanders, decided to send an army to Iceland to obtain retribution.

At this time Snorri Sturluson, an Icelander, was in Norway, and hearing of the Earl's intention, went to him and discussed the matter with him and promised the Earl that he would make arrangements with his countrymen to treat the Norwegian merchants honestly. It is thought that Snorri made a secret covenant with the Earl to have Iceland annexed to Norway in order to save the Icelanders from destruction, but as the merchants were all well treated and honestly dealt with, Snorri on his arrival in Iceland gave up the idea of annexation, but the king of Norway was working for the annexation and began by interfering with certain matters that had happened.

The archbishop and the king were both trying to obtain the same object and at this time the leader of Althing and Bishop Gudmundson were at loggerheads.

Finally the king of Norway sent a summons commanding some of the leaders to appear before him in Norway, so that he could settle matters they could not agree upon among themselves. This they at that time refused to do, but when the feids had caused such intense hatred between them that there seemed no possibility of a settlement of their disputes, they appealed to him for his judgment, getting him to act as mediator.

In this way foreign leaders interfered with the government of Iceland and by purchasing control of some of the leaders, were 'e to rule the land and not only run the government, but obtain immense profits for themselves.

Sturla Sighvatson Tries to Conquer Iceland for the King of Norway.

This man went to Rome to receive remission of his sins from the Pope, for the injustice he and his father had done to Bishop Gudmund, which having received, he on his return stayed in Norway during that winter.   King Hakon Hakonson called Sturla to him and commanded him to conquer Iceland and annex it to Norway, promising to pay him well for his trouble.   He also instructed him to induce the leaders to come to Norway and while they were absent he was to conquer their constituencies.   Sturla started for home in the year 1235.

In the following year he got his men prepared for war and attacked his uncle Snerra Sturlson and his son Urokja who had been the cause of turning many of his constituents against him during his absence.   He fought with Snorra, and caused Urokja to leave Iceland and go to Norway.

In the year 1237 Sturla fought another battle with Thorleif Thordarson who was in command of a nearby constituency and was victorious.   Snorra and several other leaders had to leave the country for Norway.

Thus Sturla conquered the whole of the west quarter of the land and next turned his attention to subduing Gissur Thorvaldson, who was the wealthiest leader of the south quarter, but by co-operation with Kolbein Arnorson, the leader of the north quarter, they succeeded in vanquishing him, killing not only himself, but also his father and his brothers who were taking his part in the feud.   This occurred in the year 1238.

Norwegian Bishops.

In the year 1238, the two Icelandic Bishops (Gudmund Arason and Thorlak Thorhallason) died, and the people, as the law was at that time, elected two candidates for the vacant bishoprics, and as usual sent them to Norway to be ordained by the archbishop. But on their arrival they were refused ordination and the archbishop sent to Iceland in their stead two Norwegians by whose help he desired to obtain the annexation of Iceland to Norway.

Snorri Sturluson.

Probably the most remarkable man in Iceland, at this time, was Snorri Sturluson, who, being an erudite man, compiled a history of the Norwegian kings, from their earliest times to the year 1178, a large work, which is called "Heimskringla," (or the Globe) and in later years he wrote the 'Snorra Edda,' (of which we have already given an account,) pertaining to heathen mythology and poetry written in verse. He was a wealthy man and one of the leaders, but like many others at that time, he was a covetous man and believed in concubinage (by taking other wives of an inferior rank to himself, besides his real or legal wife, in other words a polygamist.)

At one time he occupied the position of pronouncing lawyer. He was also created a feudal noble by the king during his first visit to Norway. He was staying with the Earl Skula when news was brought to him of the death of his brother Sighvat and his son Sturla. Snorri asked the earl to allow him to go home, which request the earl was pleased to grant. So Snorri made all preparations necessary for his return to Iceland. About the time however that he was ready to start he received a communication from the king forbidding him to leave the country, but in defiance of this Snorri said 'I will go' and sailed for his native land. Snorri at that time was not aware that any person who was a member of the feudal nobility had to receive the king's sanction before he could leave Norway, and on doing so without permission incurred the penalty of the law, also recognizing the fact that he would never be able to obtain that permission unless he gave his word to assist in the annexation of Iceland to Norway, and concluded that he would disobey the king's command, as he knew that the king was the instigator and cause of the death of Sturla and Sighvat. This action of his so incensed the king that he wrote and sent a letter to Gissur Thorvaldson, telling him to see that Snorri was sent back to Norway or failing that to have him killed.

Gissur kept this letter secret and informed no one of his intentions, but one night he left his home with 70 men and proceeded cautiously to Reykholt, the residence of Snorri, and surprised Snorri, who was totally unprepared for defence in his bedroom and murdered him. Snorri was 63 years old when he was assassinated.

The Leaders and the King's Intervention.

Some time after the events just related, a great feud sprang up between Thordar Sighvatson and Kolbeins the younger, and after the decease of Kolbeins, he fought a great battle with Brand (a relative of Kolbeins) and became the leader after he had killed Brand.

By this time Thordur and Gissur had become the most influential and wealthy leaders in Iceland and they commanded the whole of the Republic. But they could not agree on several matters and so they concluded to appeal to the King of Norway to act as mediator and left Iceland to visit the king. But as the king desired to annex Iceland to Norway he gave them very little satisfaction, and so he ordered Thordur to take the reins of government in hand and endeavor to induce the country to become subservient to the throne of Norway and pay taxes to the king. Accordingly Thordur returned to Iceland and stayed there three years, purchasing during that time the chief portion of the land, giving him the ruling power, not so much for the king as for his own aggrandizement. So the king ordered him to return to Norway. All this time the king had caused Gissur to remain in Norway and on Thordur's return, he ordered Gissur to go to Iceland for the same object as Thordur had been there before. He therefore returned home and he also governed the country more for himself than for the king, so that the bishop forced him to return to Norway in the year 1254.

For the third time the king sent yet another, a highly respectable man, whose name was Ivar Englassen, to Iceland for the same object, but he met with such a determined opposition that he only obtained power over one county in the north quarter, in the neighborhood of a bishop, who was an ardent worker for annexation. A few of the farmers agreed to pay the taxes to the king and Ivar threw the blame on Gissur's friends for his non-success on his return to Norway. So that the king as a last resort sent Thordur again to Iceland. But he only lived till 1256.

Earl Gissur and the Last of the Republic.

So the king considered it best to send Gissur and as an earnest, created the title of Earl of Iceland, which he bestowed on Gissur. But after Gissur's arrival in Iceland, instead of acting in accordance with his instructions, which were to tax the people and force them to pay them, he did not do so. The king thinking that by giving the title to Gissur it would increase his desire to rule the people and force them to obey his commands.

On arrival Gissur informed all the Icelanders of the title the king had bestowed on him, but did not mention the agreement he had made with the king regarding annexation to the Icelanders In fact he did not endeavor to promulgate the king's desire, but rather endeavored to gain as much as he could for his own aggrandizement, at the same time the king had sent several men to spy upon his actions, and one in particular, named Hallvard, a trusty man, who should endeavor to force Gissur to fulfill his compact. He informed the people at large of the agreement between Gissur and the king of Norway and some of the leading men sided with Hallvard. But Gissur had made so many friends that they all met and concluded to offer the king a considerable sum of money to absolve Gissur from his promise, on condition that they would not be beholden to the king, after his acceptance, for the payment of any further taxes nor did they wish to be in any way subservient to the king. This Hallvard refused to accept and with the co-operation of Earl Gissur attended Althing in the year 1262 and succeeded in passing the vote for annexation for the north, west and south quarters. But the eastern quarter held out until the year 1264. These people being of a more peaceable turn of mind finally agreed to pay the taxes to save bloodshed and thus the complete annexation of Iceland was accomplished and passed as law by Althing.

Times had changed since. King Olaf had first tried to annex Iceland, for at this time the people were much engaged in petty feuds which in order to obtain a settlement of, they were constantly going to Norway to ask the king to mediate between them, thus giving him a better opportunity for annexation.

A General View of the Situation of Iceland in Relation to Norway and Denmark.

It certainly is very disastrous to a nation when its leaders become so blind as to the consequences accruing, and are so anxious for their own aggrandizement, that they barter away their civic rights, political liberty and autonomy as our forefathers did during the Sturla century just mentioned.

When the nation lost the right of self-government the outlook was decidedly gloomy and the energy displayed in early times gradually faded away, for the nation had but a gloomy outlook for its future; even in ancient times matters had seldom anything but a sullen look and only on the occasion of some strenuous person addressing the people, on some subject of vital importance, did by his eloquence, and as it were inspired imagination, succeed in interesting them and throw a ray of sunshine through the clouds of indifference.

It is an interesting fact that in becoming cognizant of the ancient history of Iceland, one notes how, against immense odds, so many of the natives were able to obtain so good an education and were almost inspired. For example, take the Psalmody of Hallgrim Peterson, which was written during the most illiterate and superstitious century, or the able manner in which, we read, the Rev. Bjorn Halderson, of Sandlauksdal conducted his farming experiments, but such facts as these were exceedingly rare.

But in later years about 1760, when Icelandic affairs were in a better condition, a few of the best men visited other countries and found that their nation was far behind the times and with regret saw the backwardness of the nation and tried their best to improve the condition of the country and awake the people from their lethargy and by their superior knowledge and forethought considerably brightened the period in which they lived.

Tne First Period, 1264-1402 The Norwegian Clergy Ruled Iceland.—The Ancient Covenant.

The annexation of Iceland by Norway was consummated and the people called the document drawn up between the two nations the Ancient Covenant, and it was generally accepted.

The Norwegian kings demanded that all farmers should pay them a tax in return for their promulgating peace throughout the country and agreed to respect the laws of Iceland, for the Icelanders having nothing to do with the tariff, which they used to pay Norway, and they were given the same right as Norwegian farmers. The latter part of the covenant contains a passage which states that 'So long as the king does not break the statute himself, the people of Iceland agree to follow its dictates.' It was also stated that one Earl should reside in the country, as long as he remained true to the king and kept peace and order in the land. When however Gissur died, which occurred in 1268 this appointment ceased, and the king elected two representatives to rule Iceland and one Hrafn Oddson, became a great leader.

A New Constitution in Iceland.

The Icelanders faithfully kept to the ancient code, which was called 'Gragas,' but King Magnus Hakonarson, who was a learned jurisprudent, desired to amalgamate the few codes extant at that time in Norway,(the country then being divided into four quarters.

with a separate code of laws for each quarter) and for n one set of laws for all including also Iceland. The king therefore sent over a book, which was called 'Ironside,' because it was the usage in olden times to bind books in Iron. This book of rules and laws was accepted by Althing. The book was small but perfect, the old code being discarded. The administration was changed and in place of their having the pronouncing lawyer at their head. A lawyer, by name of Sturla Thordarson, the famous historical writer, of whom we have already heard, was the first to rule over Althing. At a later date two lawyers were appointed, one for eastern and southern quarters and one for the northern and western quarters. The rule of the ancient leaders was then abolished, and men called the 'King's Bailiffs' governed the land. The most of the rules of the quarter courts and the grand jury were abolished and all matters of law were decided by a committee of 36, who were appointed as a judicial committee. This code, however, proved unsatisfactory, both to the king and to the Icelandic population, and as he wrote another for the special government of Iceland and called it Jons' Book, he sent it by one Jons Eing, together with a man by the name of Locin, as a king's commissioner. But after having heard the contents of this new law book they found they could not agree to accept the law as a whole. But the king's commissioner in speaking before Althing, said that he thought the people had great presumption in endeavoring to make their own laws when they were already subservient to the king and he alone was fit to make laws for them. But they in reply said that they could not approve of the work, as a whole, as it would cause them to lose their liberty altogether. However, after a long discussion they agreed to approve of the new laws in part. This agreement was made at Althing in 1821, and was for many years the accepted ruling for all judicial and national affairs and some of the rulings and laws were in force today.

During the years that the book was in force foreign power over Iceland was much increased, the king having to accept laws made at Althing. But Althing had also to accept laws made by the king.

anc sonetines Altning nade laws irrespective of any interference)y tie king. As tie king's power increasec so tie power of Altning dininisiec,)tt otierwise tie law renainec ajott tie sane as tiat nace)y tie)ook 'Ironsices' anc tie old netiod of civicing the lanc into cistricts was tie origin of tie police nagistrate constituencies (cr cistricts) of tie present cay. Bailiffs were appointec as rilers, police nagistrates anc revente officers and tie governor was ciief of tie revente officers.

The Clergy Power.

In 1269 Bisiop Thorlak, who was orcainec as Bisiop of Skal- iolt, was an energetic nan, anc ie askec tie arciisiop to give iin authority to rile tie circies anc iancle all tieir property, but tie farners tioigit ie was nct treating tien justly anc was trying to ceprive tien of tieir constitutional rigits, tie)isiop claining tie rigit of tie clergy anc circi to tie fundanental system of govern- nent, wiile tie farners anc leacers ield to tie original stattes oi tieir forefatiers and tie later constitutional ame·dments, tiey iaving always tsec tie profit accured fron tie real estate attaciec to tie circies for tieir cwn)enefit.

One notaʒle case tie)isiop)roigit)efore Althing was relative to a large real estate callec Occi, wiici tie owners iac always con- trollec, tie)isiop claining it for tie circi, wiile tie owners cis- puted iis clain. Bit after a long anc arctots trial, wiich lastec fcr a longer perioc tian it woilc otierwise iave cone, owing to tie excellent nanner in wiici it was iancled by Rafn Oddson. Fie)isiop's argtnents were not generally acceptec)y Althing, so tie bischop placec iis case)efore tie arciisiop, wiile tie farners preferrec to nake tieir plea cirect to the king, anc)y agreenent)etween tien)oti, it was agreec in 1297, tiat Bisiop Arni sietlc have connanc of all tie ciocese wiici were acttal circi property. But all circi sees or real estate wiici)elongec wiolly or in lar- ger part to tie farners sioilc)e tieir incivictal property,)tt tiat they siotld pay tie sane anotnt of tax as they iac before, to tie)isiopric. Bisiop Arni was tnaɔle to oɔtain as nici as ie desired, but the power of the church over state increased considerably. He advocated and brought before Althing a new code, called 'Christians' Rights Code' and the greater part was accepted by Althing in the year 1275.

Bishop Arni was therefore the founder and instigator of the immense power and wealth the church eventually gained and held till the 16th century, at which time owing to outside causes the religion of the country was changed.

The King Makes Additional Claims.

In the year 1286 King Eirik sent one of the priests to summon 40 men from each of the four quarters, to act as soldiers and fight for him against Sweeden.

But a man named Rafn Oddson, the head lawyer at that time, called his friends together and in spite of all the bishop could do (and although a few were willing to obey the summons) they succeeded in preventing the consumm··· n of the king's order, which would have taken 160 of the best ··· f the island to other countries for military purposes.

When Hakon Magnuson became king of Norway he sent over a man, by the name of Alfur, with two commissioners, who were lawyers, but the people refused to recognize the king, so the lawyers returned empty handed at that time, but in a year later, on condition that the king agreed not to deprive them of their right according to Ancient Statutes, agreements, and also the Book of Laws which were authorized in 1302, so that (with the exception of a few Danish lawyers in the 18th century) all lawyers in Iceland were natives of the island.

A few years later the king again sent Alfur, demanding acknowledgement, and he narrowly escaped death, had not one of the leaders saved him. This happened in the year 1306.

Althing refused to accept the king's demands, and the people assembled in the south quarter to defend their country, in defence of their rights and beyond a doubt the other quarters would have cooperated with then for the public weal. Consequently Alfur found it impossible to enforce the king's decree at that time, so gave up the case entirely.

Bad Government and Hostility.--The Land Rented.

The fourteenth and fifteenth centuries saw turbulent and troublesome times, caused by a bishop, Arni Aslakson, who was a Norwegian and was ordained in 1342. He was appointed to the see of Holun and ruled over it tyranically, extorting money and other property from the people. Men fought with one another, killing and robbing with impunity, and consequently times were very hard during these centuries. All bishops who occupied the see of Holun were foreigners up to the year 1520 and at the see of Skalholt till 1466. This fact caused a great deal of trouble, for they oppressed the people by demanding large amounts of money and they lived in the most luxurious manner and but few attended to their duties as they should, except Bishop Vilckin, of Skalholt, in the year 1400, who made permanent rules of action for the district.

The bishops were not entirely to blame for the disorders and excesses, which occurred during the 14th century, for the people themselves were no better than the bishops in their dealings. About the year 1354 land was first rented. The tennants collected all taxes on them and paid the king the rent, as contracted for with him, and being anxious to make all they could out of the land, they utilized the power with which they were invested to rob the people unlawfully, so that the people often got together and either killed them or sent them away into exile.

At the latter part of the 14th century criminal cases were excessive and in many cases, especially when the government wished to get rid of certain opposition, it did not stop at showing its animosity towards the individual or party, but would rob and murder by the connivance of blood-thirsty emissaries. The church also amassed great wealth and power and it is to be regretted that they misapplied it.

Danish Rule in Iceland.

During the period in which Olaf Hakonarson ruled as king of Norway, his mother governed Denmark as Queen Margaret. While Olaf was a child Norway and Iceland were ruled by Queen Margaret with the assistance of the head governor of Norway. Olaf died at an early age in 1387. After his death Norway and Iceland were annexed to Denmark, but very few changes were made in the government of Iceland. Queen Margaret looked upon Iceland as the part of her kingdom which was to supply provisions for the king and also endeavored to secure a larger amount of revenue than usual, and accordingly sent a man over to obtain more money. But the farmers resented the action, and but for the intervention of the then governor of Iceland, Vigfus Ivarson, who was much beloved by the people, she would not have succeeded at all, but through his advice the people paid a portion of the amount demanded.

The second period (as it is called) commenced in the year 1402 and ended in the year 1550. During this period the bishops lost their control of Iceland and the stock and inhabitants on the island were devastated by a great plague.

Several times during the 'Settling century' volcanic eruptions occurred in the country and were the cause of much want and suffering amongst the inhabitants, resulting on many occasions to famine. But never before were the people driven to such straights as in the 15th century, when on many occasions food and provender for man and beast were so scarce that many died from sheer starvation. For at that time the imports consisted of small shipments from outside countries and were not sufficient for even the bare necessities of the people and their stock. With this exception the country was immune from epidemics until the 15th century, when the black plague raged all over the island. The first intimation the people had of the existence of such a disease, as the black plague, was in the year 1402 and for a period of three years was the land stricken. It is thought that it was some cloth, innoculated with the disease, which had been brought to the country in a trading vessel was the cause.

This plague raged all over Iceland and was so virulent that many farms and in some cases whole districts, were depopulated and neither before nor after this period, was such terrific havoc caused in the land. In fact, real estate was at such a low ebb that farms and property could be bought for little or nothing. In many cases those who lived through the ordeal took over the land of their relatives and neighbors, and consequently ere many years elapsed many men became wealthy land owners.

Matters were however soon straightened out and the pluck and energy of the Icelanders was much thought of abroad.

The Commerce of the Country.

As the climate of Iceland prevents the growing of much grain and timber is exceedingly scarce, the people had to depend on foreign countries for their supply of breadstuffs, iron, lumber, coal, salt and many other commodities. The chief industries of Iceland are: Salted codfish, of which large quantities are exported, coldliver oil, seal oil, whale oil, shark oil, wool, butter, a limited supply of woollen goods, sealskins and sheepskins. In early times the trading was entirely in the hands of the Icelanders, for which they received remunerative profits, while later on the Norwegians had a share of it. But gradually Icelandic commerce dwindled down to almost nothing and was chiefly in the hands of Norwegians, until at last the king of Norway was considered the master and of commerce and accordingly in the year 1300 the king handed over to the Norwegian merchants of Bergen the rights of Icelandic commerce, which they continued to hold for a long time.

About the year 1400 English ships sailed to Iceland, sent out on account of the excellent fisheries surrounding the coast and also with the idea of trading with the people. They bought more and presumably paid a better price than the Norwegians, but were of such a warlike disposition that they were continually fighting with the islanders, robbing them of their live stock, spoiling their fishing gears and creating pillage, rapine and murder. But in the year 1434, a pitched battle was fought and the Icelanders were victorious.

The king of Norway and the Bergen merchants finding that commercial relations between them and the Icelanders was suffering by the inroads of the English traders, prohibited the English from trading with Iceland, issuing orders to that effect to the governor and commanded him to see that his orders were obeyed by both Icelanders and English. On one occasion an Icelandic governor was captured by the English and taken to England.

Finally the king of Denmark made an arrangement by which they were allowed to trade with Iceland, by paying a certain amount of taxes. But owing to the evasion of the English of paying the import duty, the hostilities continued.

The governor, who was mentioned above as having been captured by the English, was named Bjorn the wealthy, and he had such bitter feelings towards the English, that he by the king's orders forced them to pay customs duty, which so incensed the English that they murdered him.

His wife, who was a woman of determined mind, ordered her men and obtained the help of her friends and raised a force which contended with the English and killed nearly all of them.

During the 16th century the Germans began to trade with Iceland, which caused a great animosity between them and the English, as their goods could be bought by the Icelanders for less than the English could supply them for. Consequently during the early part of the 16th century, the feud caused them to open hostilities and resulted in victory for the Germans and they forced the English to leave the port.

The Overbearing Conduct of the Bishops.

During the 11th and 12th centuries the bishops endeavored to increase the desire for better knowledge and a more amicable feeling

44

between the various factions and by means of her priests the church
endeavored to not only educate, but also provide help for and encour-
age the poor and also care for the sick, the people subscribing an
amount sufficient to support the cause. Naturally the bishops were the
ruling power in such cases and did a great deal of good.   Consequently with the advance of education times were changed and the
church, holding sway over the minds of the people, imposed upon
them the acts of confession and penance, which was naturally looked
upon as severe, especially in relation to matrimony, which forbade
the clergy and persons related as far as the 5th in cousinship to
marry, and many objected to being subservient to penance, which in
several cases especially among the wealthier class, caused great re-
sentment as if occasion was presumed requisite, their property was
confiscated or punishment by imprisonment, flogging or excommuni-
cation inflicted.   If the offence was not of a severe nature they
were religated to walk barefooted to the church from their residence
and stand at the church door (no matter what the weather would be)
until mass was over.   By this you can notice that the power of the
bishops not only in judicial matters, but in temporal affairs greatly
increased.   In the years elapsing between the 14th and 15th centuries unfortunately the bishops did not take pains to educate the
people or use their influence to create good feelings or peacable mo-
tives amongst them. They lived in a luxurious manner and although
presumably living a quiet life, they at the same time used all their
influence in extorting money from the inhabitants of their respective
districts and whenever they could do so penitents were mulched in
sums of money in the most over-bearing manner.

In the year 1433, Jon Geirekson, a Norwegian and bishop, (who
through his excesses and debaucheries was forced to resign his
bishopric in Norway,) was appointed by the king, (who was very
indifferent in his feeling to Iceland) who concluded that he was
the right party to send there.   The king of Denmark, by name Eirik
of Pommern, in spite of the fact that Jon was the archbishop of Up-
psolum in Sweeden, gave him an escort of 30 servants and had
him ordained as bishop at Skalholt.   His men, however, killed

by his orders, one of the leaders which caused so much ill feeling and hatred between them and the people, that they, after killing all his retinue, and after having tied him in a sack, threw him into a river and consequently he was drowned.

In the years 1450-1520, Olaf and Gottskalk, who were bishops residing at Holum, were known to be the most merciless and overbearing bishops that Icelanders ever knew. Olaf, for little or no reason, excommunicated one of the wealthiest farmers, who owned at that period 100 farms, and at the same time passed the same sentence on the pronouncing lawyer.

Bishop Gottskalk became very much richer in lands and money than Olaf. He was a man capable of horrible atrocities, and was called 'Gottskalk the merciless.' One of his worst acts was the persecution of a farmer named Jon Sigmundson, a very rich man, who he contended had married his fourth cousin, but Jon brought sufficient evidence to prove that this was an untruth and proved his innocence of the charge before the people. But notwithstanding all this the bishop confiscated all his property and wealth. The Icelanders were so incensed at this that they combined and agreed to see that not only their rights should be respected but banded together to defend their property against the clerical powers. This event happened in the year 1513.

Indulgences and Protestants.

In the year 1517 a cardinal, sent out by Pope Leo 10th, arrived in Iceland, he having been commissioned to collect all the money he could for the purpose of raising funds for the building of the cathedral of St. Peter, at Rome, which is now the most magnificent and stately building erected in the world and many millions of dollars have been spent in beautifying the edifice exteriorly and in its interior. He was commissioned to sell indulegnces, granting a remission of certain sins committed by members of the Catholic faith, also promising thereby to grant a lessening of punishment in the future state. The bishop of Skalholt, Stefan Jonson, in speaking to his congregation, persuaded them not to buy these indulgences.

but would not commit himself to ordering them not to, as he being a bishop dared not dispute the authority of the Pope.

The cardinal however sold a great many and consequently obtained considerable money. The churches throughout the then known world all helped to contribute towards the same object. About this time a priest by the name of Martin Luther, seceded from the Roman Catholic church and in his discourses in Europe denied the legitimability of the sale of these indulgences, stating that God alone could forgive sins. Many of the people sided with him and consequently a new religion called Lutheran, was created and these people were called Protestants, in contra distinction to Roman Catholicism.

In those countries where the reformers had the upper hand the king confiscated all the church property, benifices, cloisters and real estate belonging to the bishops, but was generous enough to provide for the education of the children and the care of the sick and needy. By this time the reformers had abolished the worship of saints and allowed the clergy the right of marriage.

The Reformation in Skalholt.

In the year 1530, Christian the III. became king of Denmark, and approved of the tenets of reformation and in the year 1537, he sent to Iceland a man by the name of Klaus, who was well received by the Icelanders, and in the year 1538 the king caused to be sent to Iceland a statement concerning the government of the churches and the method of conducting the services and other parochial matters, being the same law governing that body in Denmark. The Roman Catholic Bishop of Skalholt, Ogmundson and Jon Arason, the bishop at Holum, refused to have anything to do with the matter.

In the year 1540 an Icelander, by the name of Oddur and his friend, who were highly educated men, and who were residing in Germany, translated the New Testament into the Icelandic language. This work was printed in Denmark 1540.

The bishop of Skalholt, who was an aged man and was becoming almost blind, desired that Gissur should be appointed to succeed him, who, when he was in Denmark, (to which country he had to go to be ordained) promised the king to become a convert to the new religion and follow its tenets and on his arrival in Iceland took his seat at Althing as a bishop. But in the same year he had already made a promise to rule the churches according to the old regime. However, on his taking his seat he endeavored to introduce the new laws in relation to clerical matters at Althing. But the bishop of Holum, Jon Arason, refused to have anything to do with it.

During the time that Gissur was in Denmark a man, by the name of Didrik, who held a government commission, was killed at Skalholt, owing to the fact that on Whitsunday, of 1540, he had driven all the people out of the monastery at Videy. But the Abbé, or head man at Skalholt, caused him to be executed. The vice-governor, who was ruling during the absence of the governor, however, thought that the bishop was in some way or other responsible for this act of Dridrik's. On the king hearing of this matter, he also turned against the bishop and issued credentials accusing the bishop of the fact, which he dispatched to Iceland, to be brought up in Althing. But the people having duly considered the matter dismissed the accusation.

The newly appointed Bishop Gissur in endeavoring to introduce the new religious ideas, promulgated by the reformation, into his district, consisting of the omission of some of the old forms and the method of performing divine service, hearing that the old bishop whose see he had taken over desired in conjunction with the then bishop of Holum, to fight against the introduction of these new doctrines, took the necessary steps to stop this interference with his ideas and the matter was allowed to go on and as far as can be ascertained, Bishop Gissur was the cause of the Danish governor, by the name of Christofer Hvitfeld, coming over to Iceland in the year 1546, with two war vessels to arrest the old bishop Ogmund, who was nearly blind, confiscating all his property.

During the summer of the same year the Althing approved of
the introduction of Lutheranism, Bishop Jon being the only one not
present, sending a letter, informing the assemblage that he only
felt justified in obeying the king under the old covenant.

Through the efforts of Gissur Lutheranism became popular in
Skalholt with a few but not amongst the people and even the priests
preferred to resign rather than embrace the new regime, although
the bishops had started a school for the instruction of the clergy.

Bishop Gissur died at the age of 40, in 1548.

Bishop Jon Arason.

Bishop Jon Arason was, if not the most, at least a very remarkable man in Iceland at this time. He was a skilful, ambitious, fanatical, energetic and an excellent leader of the old style. He wrote
a few poems which were considered fairly good, but he was not a
highly educated man. After he had become a priest, he, like many
other priests at this period, took a concubine into his home, with
whom he lived and by whom he had six children. In the early days
this was often done, as the law forbade them to marry.

One of the best things he did was to introduce into Iceland a
printing press which he caused to be sent to the town of Holum in
1524.

Bishop Jon was a firm believer in the Roman Catholic religion
and used his utmost efforts to prevent the introduction of Lutheranism into his diocese. After the death of Bishop Gissur he endeavored to gain command of the bishopric of Skalholt. But a Revd.
John Bjarnson, who was a Lutheran, defended his position, so for
the present Bishop Jon could do no more. During the year 1549
Bishop Jon was ordered to go to Denmark to meet the king, but the
bishop refused to, so he was ordered by the king on account of dis-
obeying his command, to go into exile.

The same summer however, he received a mandate from the
Pope of Rome, to remain in Iceland, sending him his blessing and

commanded him to protect Roman Catholicism at all costs, even to lighting for it if necessary.

The bishop was exceedingly pleased when he received these instructions and determined to fight for the church and its right. The first idea was protection of what he had, so he erected a line of forts around the bishopric of Holum. He next sent his sons to arrest Bishop Martin, of Skalholt, whom he put in prison at Holum.

In the summer of 1550 he marched with a large army to Althing, and Althing had to submit to any rules or laws he made. He then marched to Skalholt and took it into his possession. After this he went to Videy, at which place he drove out all the Danes who were in the monastery and restored order there according to the old regime. On the way he did the same thing at Helgalfell.

The following autumn he went to Saudafell, with the intention of capturing a farmer named Dada Gudmundson, of Snoskdal, an active adherent of the king's. But Dada having got together a body of picked men, surprised the bishop and his sons and made them prisoners. Dada took them to Skalholt with the intention of keeping them there until the next Althing met, but the governor being afraid that they might either escape or be rescued desired to have them executed at once. Consequently Bishop Jon and his sons were beheaded on the 7th of November, 1550.

During the winter following the bishop's adherents killed the governor and many Danes also.

The 3rd Period, From 1550—1683. Kingly Power and Monopoly.

After the death of the bishop resistance to the introduction of Lutheranism ceased, and the following summer the king sent over three war vessels and by this means caused the ordinances of reformation to be accepted by the whole population and Bishop Jon and his sons were pronounced traitors, and no one had the energy or power to defend this accusation. After this a great many changes took place in the country. The power of the bishops was diminished, while to a small extent that of the Islanders increased. But the king accrued more power than ever as he confiscated all real estate belonging to the monasteries, churches and that of those who fought against the introduction of Lutheranism; consequently about one-fifth of all real estate was appropriated to the king's use and the greater portion of rents, taxes, &c., went to fill the king's exchequer. He also appointed bailiffs. These 'King's Bailiffs' could impress the people to work without pay when they wished them to. A bailiff held a position similar to a 'water bailiff' of the present day, but their powers were not so limited; consequently only those residing in the immediate neighborhood of the sea were affected, he having fishing boats called 'king's boats.' (These were originally captured from the German merchants.) But in many cases the bailiffs owned boats of their own, and being avaricious, called these also 'king's boats' and thus they extorted considerable wealth from the people.

Some of the foreign bishops who had acquired considerable wealth took some of it away. But as a rule they preferred to get as much as they could for the church and their own aggrandizement. But the comparatively small amount paid as tribute to the Pope did little towards impoverishing the country.

After the king had confiscated the wealth and thus crippled the power of the church it became necessary to provide for schools, the sick and the needy. So in the year 1552 it was decided to have one school at Skalholt and another at Holt which were to be provided for and provisioned by the tax on real estate belonging to the church, and were founded especially for the purpose of improving conditions and providing for the clergy.

Legislative Power and Constitution.

After the reformation the king and his bailiffs were more particular in seeing after the laws of the land and on many occasions Althing was very fraudulently dealt with and laws and regulations were passed which caused a great amount of dissatisfaction amongst the people, more especially as they could not cope against a foreign power. This Governor Pall was enabled in the year 1564, to cause to be passed by coertion at Althing, an approval of a code of penal laws, with which the people were much dissatisfied.

This code related to immoral cases, such as fornication, adultery, consanguinity in marriage and other such matters.

This code was at that time in force in Denmark, so the king of Denmark, Frederick the Second, desired that the governor should have it enforced in Iceland.

In the year 1563 the king ordered the governor to appoint a jury of 24 men and commanded that he should inspect all verdicts given by the court and see that they were properly drawn up and right. Before this time no person except the king was allowed to change their verdicts. Thirty years later in 1593 a grand jury was established. This act of the king was intended to diminish the power of Althing.

Bishop Gudbrand Thorlakson.

Nothing remarkable can be said of any of the bishops who were in Iceland during the period between the years 1550 and 1570, but in the following year, 1571, one of the most energetic men ever reigning as a bishop in Iceland, was ordained at Holt. This was Bishop Gudbrand. He purchased the press, printing materials and other things connected with it, that Bishop Jon Arason had brought some years before to Holt and having purchased new supplies for it, he established a printing office and published many works for the education both of the clergy and the people. His most remarkable work was a copy of the Bible which he translated. This work was so perfect in every respect and so well got up that every Icelander looks upon it with pride. This Bible he produced in the year 1584 and is to be seen in our library at Reykjavik.

Thus the people were enabled not only to read, or at any rate hear it read, in their own language, and it consequently influenced their religious education to a great extent. But of course education was really in its infancy at that time and the minds of the common people, especially were thoroughly fanatical in their superstitious beliefs, so bigoted, so little given to thinking or reasoning of either humanity or Christianity, that it is small wonder, although we very much regret the fact that Bishop Gudbrand spent a large portion of his lifetime in law suits and persecution. At the same time the bishop was not honest either to himself or to the people, from the fact that he honored the influence and power of the king while he disrespected the power of the Althing, he desiring that the church should rule in all religious matters.

However, a lawyer, Jon Jonson, defended the people's rights at Althing. He was, however, a very bad man, taking part as accuser in penal laws and was continually censuring some one or objecting to some law or action. Bishop Gudbrand wishing to improve the condition of the clergy, many of whom were in straightened circumstances, wrote to the king, and so interested him in the cause that he sent 100 rikisdalirs (equal to 50 dollars) a year for their benefit. The bishop of Skalholt, hearing of this, also applied, and the king kindly agreed to give his diocese the sum of 200 rikisdalirs (equal to 100 dollars) as there were so many more in this see that were in need of assistance.

Through all of Bishop Gudbrand's life he devoted much of his time to the education (by publishing books) of the people and had an able assistant in his cousin, Arngrim, who was greatly instrumental in teaching them also. He was a well educated and a well read man, writing many works about Iceland and also the history of the country in Latin, in fact his writings were much read by the learned men of foreign lands and it is known to be a fact that many became interested in the history and folklore of Iceland. Arngrim died in the year 1648.

In the year 1630 Bishop Odd, of Skalholt, also died, and he like Arngrim, had also written many valuable manuscripts relative to the same subjects.

Bishop Gudbrand died during the year of 1627 at the ripe old age of 85.

Commercial Monopoly.

After the discovery of America the prices for Icelandic commodities largely increased owing to a greater demand caused by the extension of trade and consequently the people were very much benefited.

During the 16th century most of the trading with Iceland was done by foreigners who were principally English, Germans or Hollanders and during the latter part of the century was extremely beneficial to the Icelanders.

At this time, however, commercial complications between the rulers of the various countries caused each of them to strive for the protection of their own merchants and do all they could towards obtaining the greater share of the trade; consequently they issued 'letters patent' giving their own traders special rights and privileges.

King Christian, the Fourth, of Denmark, however, as Iceland was a dependancy of his, concluded to take this opportunity to protect the Danish trade, so he granted the Danish merchants 'letters patent,' allowing them the sole right and privilege to trade with Iceland, and stated that he thought it was not justifiable that foreigners should have the benefit instead of himself.

This monopoly, with but a few changes, continued for a period of 250 years. The king, although protecting his Danish subjects, did not endeavor to cause the Icelanders to suffer by this monopoly, but ordered the traders that they should carry nothing but good and carefully prepared produce and demanded of them that they should do their duty, by obeying the instructions he had issued. But as he had appointed no inspectors to oversee the latter and see that justice was done many unscrupulous merchants sometimes brought damaged produce. Consequently foreign produce advanced in price, while the Icelandic was not affected and remained the same. The Icelanders soon found out that trade was suffering from this cause, so they appealed to the king for protection from these unscriptlots merchants and in the year 1619 he officially caused fixed prices to be given for the sale and barter of all commodities that they and the traders dealt in. The dealers, however, were very much dissatisfied at this and finally were enabled to have the price list changed for the benefit of their own interest.

The king's decree required the merchants to call at twenty harbors, situated at different places around Iceland. But on but few occasions, sometimes for years, they did not go near the smaller ones, owing to the fact that they could make a greater profit by going to the larger ports. In the year 1662 the king had the island divided into four sections or commercial districts. These he rented to a company of merchants and made them pay the sum of 50,000 rikisdalirs, a sum equivalent to 25,000 dollars, which was an exceedingly large amount of money in those days, considering the company had to make enough out of their trading to pay for their business expenses and also obtain sufficient to pay a profit.

This manner in which the land was divided, or rather having it divided at all, was a great mistake on the part of the king, as many of the farmers were obliged to travel long distances to their trading point, where otherwise they were a great deal nearer some other port and it was extremely hard to be compelled to do so, as in case of non-compliance with the statute a heavy penalty was incurred.

Foreign Pirates.

At the time that so many nations had their ships sailing in the North Sea. Iceland was always in great danger from the frequency of piratical vessels sailing in that vicinity. So a police magistrate, by the name of Magnus Jonson, asked the king to let him have arms and munitions of war, so that he could teach the icelanders military tactics, at that time being devoid of any arms for defence of the Island, but although it would no doubt in many instances have assisted them, the king refused his request.

In the year 1627 the people suffered most from piratical attacks. This year four Turkish war vessels, thoroughly equipped with arms and ammunition and manned by a crew of malevolent, desperate, blood-thirsty, merciless men, who being Moslems hated Christians, arrived at Grindavik on the south part of the island and robbed the place. From there they went to Bersastada, intending to capture two merchant vessels which were anchored in a narrow harbor, but ran ashore and were there for two days, working hard to get their ships afloat again.

Bersastadur was the governor's seat at that time and they had some obsolete cannon or large guns of some kind, but it is presumed on account of their antiquity the governor was afraid to fire them, so the pirates sailed away unhurt. The part of the country that suffered most from their depredations and rapine, was in the Westman Islands, and the eastern coast. In the Westman islands they captured 240 of the inhabitants, whom they took away and sold as slaves. Ten years later the king of Denmark paid a ransom for twenty of them. They also killed some of the people and pillaged their towns, in fact took everything of value they could. The people that were sick or wounded they put into the merchant buildings and set fire to them and burned every one in them.

On the east coast they captured 110, who they also took with them.

Witches Burned, Owing to the Superstition of the Times.

One of the darkest pages in our history was the fanatical superstition and belief in witchcraft, ascending all over the country, which became almost an epidemic during the 17th century.

The belief in the rites and orgies was introduced from foreign countries and the people were perfect fanatics in religious matters, especially during the 16th and 17th centuries, when it amounted to an almost inordinate savagery; consequently the good seed sown by the introduction of Lutheranism was checked and became stagnant. The popular belief in devils increased to such an extent, that the people really believed they could see imps and devils all around them.

Witchcraft had a terrible hold on them. If a person got sick some imp was the cause of his illness. If a horse or a cow was lost or died, imps or ghosts were blamed for it, they believing that some bad man or wicked woman had sent them. These things caused the people much apprehension. They became suspicious of each other, were nervous to a degree, in fact became half-crazy.

They would accuse a neighbor of being a magician or a woman of being a witch, until during the year 1628 one man was actually arrested and accused of calling up a ghost. He was finally burned alive. He however, was of course, really perfectly innocent of any such thing. He was an honest man and had never done any unconstitutional act. But in Denmark it was proclaimed as a lawful act to torture and burn such men and women. Some years later in the 17th century, twenty men were convicted of witchcraft and burned at the stake. But thanks to the efforts of Christofer Herdeman, burning for witchcraft was abolished in the year 1690.

This article has, I trust, clearly shown what atrocities can be committed where ignorance and superstition gets a hold on a nation.

Bishop Brynjolf Sveinson and Hallgrim Peterson.

Bishop Brynjolf, of Skalholt, was ordained in the year 1639, and continued his work there for 35 years. He was a man of great executive ability and was given charge of all the finances of the church and amassed quite a fortune of his own. In the latter years of his life a great calamity befel him, so he appointed another bishop to assist him and some time after resigned. He died in the year 1675 at the age of 70 years. He was celebrated during his lifetime for being an erudite man. He was conversant of and could speak both the Greek and Latin languages and was well posted in our national history and language also and was possessor of a great many of the most valuable books and manuscripts. King Frederick the Third, who was then the Danish ruler, desired to make him his historian, but this offer the bishop refused to accept. So the king being desirous of obtaining some of his books and documents for his own library, asked the bishop for the m, and in accordance with the king's wish sent a celebrated manuscript of pcems, belonging to the 13th century, called 'Somundar Edda,' also the 'Flateyau Book,' a large history written in the 14th century and in addition some other very valuable works.

The bishop was a great leader and succeeded in raising 50,000 rikisdalirs (equal to 25,000 dollars) to build a cathedral at Skalholt. He was also desirous of establishing a printing office there. But the bishop at Holum who was an illiterate man, prevented him from doing so.

His funeral sermon was preached by Hallgrim Peterson, which begins with the words, 'Man is but a flower,' which is used at all funerals in Iceland today, and has been translated into many languages.

Hallgrim Peterson was a priest for 25 years at Saurby; he was a poor man and in straightened circumstances, and during the last eight years of his life he became a leper and consequently had to employ ancther priest to take charge of his parish and shortly afterwards resigned. He died at the age of 60, in the year 1674.

He was most famous as a poet and more especially in composing hymns. He was a man of visionary ideas, rich in grand and beautiful thoughts. His artlessness accorded admirably with the imagery of his imagination and his sincerity with his belief in Chrstianity.

Both the bishop and himself were single-minded in their belief of the Christian doctrine, which can easly be seen by reading his hymns. When he became stricken with leprosy, that dread disease, he found great consolation in the thought of all Christ suffered in comparison to the small amount of suffering we have to bear and he liked to compare human life with that of the Savior's.

Many of his hymns were written relative to the life of Christ and have been the means of affecting and improving the religious feeling of the people. His hymns have been printed more than 40 times, besides many of his other hymns and poems are to be found amongst the people all over the island.

Both he and the bishop, Brynjolf, lived during the times when witchcraft spread over the land. But they were not only averse to it but did all they could to suppress it. Bishop Brynjolf was esteemed and honored by his country on account fo his erudition. He could see whether a man was clever or not and would assist him. He took a fancy to and aided Hallgrim Peterson in his studies and finally ordained him as a priest. But after all, the beautiful inspirations of Hallgrim Peterson were as a light shining in the darkness and his hymns are considered the supreme ideal of all others the nation possesses.

The Hereditary State.

In all the years that Iceland was a dependency of Denmark, the kings were elected, but this statute was amended, when in the year 1660, the king of Denmark, Fredrick the Third, claimed the right of hereditary for his descendants and in the course of a few months was proclaimed 'Monarch' of Denmark, but still retained the title cf king of Norway, as the right of hereditary was still in force there. But in the year 1661 Norway accepted the innovation and he was proclaimed Monarch of Norway and Denmark. In the year 1662 Henrik Bjelke, who was governor of Iceland, waited until the session of Althing was over and in order to more easily get the people to swear allegiance to the king, he summoned them to come to 'Kopavogi,' where the lands men swore allegiance to the king, but the question of monarchial rule was not mentioned.

After they had sworn to this He produced a letter or rather a document, which was written in Danish, and ordered the men to affix their marks or names to it. This document was for the purpose of authorizing the monarchial right of the king and his descendants over Iceland. There were very few of the people who understood the purpose of the government and when they were informed of the deprivation of their rights against the election of the king, they objected to having their names enrolled. But Bjelke pleaded with them and explained that it would not deprive them of any of their rights, but was the rule all over the Danish kingdom. They signed their names to the document and said that they sincerely hoped the king would make good his promises through their governor.

The 4th Period, 1683 1750. Monarchy and Monopoly. Changes of Government.

In the latter part of the 17th Century, in the year 1683, monarchy and monopoly began to be a fact all over the land. Bailiffs were sent to keep order on the island and the following year, a governor over Iceland was appointed but he resided in Denmark; this was Ulfrik Christian Gyldenlove. He was the illegitimate son of King Christian the 5th and was only 15 years of age when he was appointed to the position. These governors could only be of noble birth or descent; but a Danish nobleman was not allowed to reside in Iceland, consequently they never visited the island and it was not requisite for the governor to have any acquaintance with Iceland and so it mattered not what his age might be. But in a few years later on the king thought that it would be preferable to have a governor as a resident of the island, so in the year 1688 he ordered a governor to rule over the people and reside there. He was to have command of the judicial court and of all cases which the bailiff were not entitled by the statute to act upon.

So the king accordingly appointed a man by the name of Christian Muller, a Dane, and he conducted himself in a most ludicrous manner and made a very poor governor.

All the governors of Iceland were ruled by Danish laws and had to consult the king on all matters relative to the government of the island and its inhabitants, much to the people's disgust.

The Constitution.

About the year 1688 two codes of laws were published, one for the Danes and another for the Norwegians and in the same year the king sent to the several officers ruling in Iceland, the Norwegian Code or Book of Laws, and commanded them to look over the existing code of constitutional laws then extant in Iceland and write a code of laws for the government of the people and such judicial statutes as were necessary. This they did and sent the rescript to the Danish administration. But these compilations of the law were almost useless and the various points of law were all mixed up, for the simple reason that as a law made for the Danes probably did not apply to the Norwegians or Icelanders and vice versa, each of the countries having a different code, the Icelanders petitioned the king to let them have the Norwegian law in preference to the Danish and this was presumably accepted some time later.

When Pall Vidalin, a celebrated lawyer, saw the manner in which the law had been mixed up, he worked hard to have the laws straightened out.

In the year 1736 a young man wishing to become a lawyer, had to pass an examination to obtain the right to practice and had to study at the University in Denmark and those desiring to become police magistrates had also to do the same. On going back to Iceland they found matters in a confused state, for the lawyers and magistrates used the code of laws they had studied in the University, and consequently did not become acquainted with the laws of their country. So neither they nor anyone else knew anything about the new laws as the book had never been published.

The Mission of Lawyer Gottorp.

The finances of the country were growing worse and worse. Monopoly and other causes were creating havoc and causing the people to get into lots of trouble. So they wrote an application to the king, asking him to kindly permit them to send one of their leading lawyers and commission him to acquaint his majesty with the terrible shape the financial affairs of the island were in.

This petition he granted and in the year 1701 a lawyer, by the name of Larus Gottrup, prepared for his mission to the king. The governor put so many impediments in his way and caused so much dissention between the people themselves, that his mission effected little or no good for the country and things were almost worse than before.

After this the king granted them leave to have a commissioner appointed in Copenhagen to look into the matter and try to straighten out things. But again, owing to there being so much dissention amongst themselves, they caused a great deal of hindrance and consequently not much good could be done.

However in the year 1702 the king caused a fixed price for all commodities and produce and this to some extent relieved the financial pressure existing.

After the Danish government had looked into the reports the governor had presented, they found that he had been misrepresenting the affairs of the country. His reputation was certainly not as good as it would have been, had he acted honestly with the government and the people.

Arni Magnuson and Pall Viddalin.

ARNI MAGNUSON.

The result of Gottrups mission to the king ended by the king giving instructions and a commission to Arni Magnus and Pall Viddalin, commanding them to inquire with the utmost diligence, into the exact financial condition of the country and make out a complete book of assessments of all real estate and property and also to make a complete census, that is a complete enumeration of all the lands and estates in Iceland, their quantity and worth, with numbers of the wives, children, servants, tenants or serving men that each person might have, so as to enable the king to fix the proper amount of tax due from each one; to inspect all commercial matters, in fact all political, financial or general affairs and send the result of their inquiries to the Danish government for inspection and also to state the amount of improvements, in fact a complete list of all that pertained to the country in any respect.

This work covered a period from the year 1702 to 1712. This entailed an immense amount of labor and more than they could carry out correctly, for it caused Pall Viddalin who was not what would be called a really peace-loving man, to have many law suits with the farmers and leaders and caused much dissatisfaction amongst the leading men of the country. Pall and Arni had many law suits, which of course greatly hindered their work. They however succeeded in making a census of the farm lands and other territory of the whole island, giving a full description of each farm and how many servants and hired men and how much stock they had, that is, the number of horses, cattle or sheep the farmers owned. The census was completed in the year 1703. They found the number of inhabitants to be 50,000. They also caused great improvements to be made in the condition of the tenants and had regulations printed for the guidance and manner in which they were to be treated by the landlords. They also received tenants' leases, so that they could see that their rights were protected. They also inquired into commercial matters and Arni Magnusen contested that no commercial right should be sold to one company, but that two or three different firms should do business at that point as it would, by opposition, create competition which would be of great benefit to the people.

Pall Viddalin was considered the most learned lawyer that ever was in Iceland.

But Arni Magnuson was highly cultured and thoroughly acquainted with national governmental affairs and had an intimate knowledge of the history of the nation, was a great grammarian, and had a keen sense of judgment. Before the king ordered him to Iceland, and he was privy archivist to the king and owned a very large and remarkable collection of manuscripts. During his residence in

Iceland and while employed in the business of the king, he collected as many documents and manuscripts as he possibly could and he continued to do so as long as he lived. Unfortunately some of his collection was burned, including a few of his own manuscripts, but he was luckily enabled to save the greater part from destruction. He was also the means of preventing many extremely valuable manuscripts from being taken away by foreigners, which would have been but for his interefence consequently lost to the nation.

Before he died he made a will in which he deeded all his property, works and manuscripts to the Danish university, with the express understanding that they were to be used for the aid of Icelandic students in studying the history of their country, the folklore, poetry and the laws ancient and modern.

Bishop Jon Viddalin.

Bishop Jon Viddalin held the office of bishop at Skalholt from the year 1698 till 1720. He was a very intelligent and intellectual man and an eloquent speaker; he was most noted for having written a book of sermons for the use of families, which was used for many years in home services throughout the country. In fact, it was not until Bishop Peterson wrote a book of family worship, which he had printed in the year 1856 that the use of the other was discontinued, the latter work being more up-to-date and very much plainer in its wording. Bishop Jon Vidallin was of a domineering disposition, but at the time he lived, the leaders were continually disputing, many of whom were bullying and aggressive men. A certain lawyer by the name of Odd Sigurdson, who was very popular, was responsible for many of the law-suits, as a great many of the men at that time were given to debauchery and drink. Sad to say the bishop used to drink considerably himself. But a few years later a bishop by the name of Jon Arason, took the see in charge and made great changes amongst the clergy, and by turning out of office those that were the worst drunkards, the improved the status of the church. He held office from the year 1722—1743.

Lodriks Harbo Mission.

In the 1741, through a report made to the king by Jon Thor-kellson, who had been a schoolmaster at Skalholt, of the terrible state in which the church, clergy and education was in Iceland. He deputed one of the Danish priests, the Rev. Lodrik Harboe, to re-side in Iceland, for a period of three years and commanded him to thoroughly inspect the condition of the churches, clergy and schools. and report on the state in which he found Christianity in relation to the people. As the priest was ignorant of the Icelandic language it became necessary that the king should send an interpreter with him, who should also act as his secretary, and as Jon Thorkelson had been there as a schoolmaster, the king thought he would be the best man to send. Thorkelson a few years later established an educa-tional fund called Thorkelson Fund!

When it became known by the Icelanders that Revd. Harboe was ordered to Iceland, the news caused great excitement amongst the islanders and especially were the clergy roused. Numbers of stories were circulated throughout the country. First that he was going to force them to accept the old heathen mythological rites, an-other that he would brand everyone on their foreheads who would not do his bidding and many other such nonsensical ideas. The priests and other clergy were also afraid, as they heard that he was going to speak to them and examine them in Latin and Greek, to prove as to whether they were educated or not. The people were mostly an ignorant class and naturally they believed all those foolish stories as they had poor judgment of their own.

However, after Rev. Harboe had been with them for a while, they put implicit trust in him, as he was a generous, highly educated, kind and God-fearing man.

Jon Thorkelson was, however, not much help to him, as he was his opposite in ideas, quick tempered, domineering and hard hearted, and wished to treat the people and the clergy with severity. This Harboe refused to do. Educational matters at this time were at a low ebb. He also found that the pastors were poor scholars and

ignorant and in poor circumstances. They did not have the necessary school books. The condition of the schools was bad, being in
poor situations, more especially at Holum, where Sigurdur Vigfuson,
who was called the Icelandic giant, was schoolmaster.

Revd. Harboe in the year 1743, made a new ordinance for conducting and managing the schools. There is no doubt that had the
bishops done their duty by supplying the necessary funds
to furnish good teachers and school books and other articles needed for the use of the scholars and teachers,
much good would have been done. He also introduced the rite of
confirmation of the young boys and girls, when they had learned their
catechism. This had already been introduced into the church in
Denmark. In the same year 1744, he also caused to be translated
into Icelandic, a Christian school book, which is called 'Pontoppid-
ans' and ordered the clergy to see that the children were instructed
in it. The pastors were also ordered to visit all the homes and examine the children to find out what progress they had made in their
edication and study of the Christian beliefs.

But when a generation is brought up in ignorance, hardship and
in a barbarous manner, and intellectual thought and self-will almost
unheard of, improvement comes but by slow degrees.

The king being of a religious turn of mind and desirous of bet-
tering his people, thought it possible, by issuing a penal statute
regarding edication and Christian teaching it might be of benefit, but
although some of it was of much use and no doubt necessary,
other portions and rules were not. For instance, he forbade that children should be allowed to read the history of their own country and
he had inserted many other rules that were not of much account.

The Fifth Period, 1750 to 1830. Fight Against Monopoly and Ignor-
ance. Skuli Magnuson. Commerce and Factories.

In the year 1749 Skuli Magnuson was the governor of Iceland.
He was in the prime of his life and well known for his energy and
ability and was a hard man to deal with if he met with resistance to
his will. He naturally was in a position to become better acquain-

ted with the condition of the people and other natural matters than anyone else. He thoroughly recognized the fact that the industries of the country were as yet in their infancy and that his countrymen were far behind the times.   As to cultivation there was hardly any. The dwellings were in a ruinous condition. There were not enough boats, tackle and other seafaring paraphanalia for profitable fishing.   The sheeps' wool was sold just as it was clipped from the sheep and sent abroad.   They had only the simplest forms of agricultural indus-trial and household implements and those they did have were out of date, many of them antiquated.   The existence of monopoly by the merchants for supplying the needs of the people, depressed them and not only sapped their energy but obstructed progression and hindered the advance of civilization and Christianity.   Skuli wished to awaken the people to become more industrious and endeavored to get them to work with more harmony together, with more will and courage, so he got several of the leaders together and organized a company of shareholders for the purpose of establishing a woollen factory, in spite of the fact, that he knew they would meet with great opposition from the Merchants' company and knew that he must have a charter ratified and sanctioned by the king before he endeav-ored to start up a business of that kind and thus have the factory started on a solid basis.   So in 1757 Skuli sailed for Denmark and he sent to the government a statement of the industrial condition of the country and an abstract of his company's intention, requesting the king to give him the right to traffic and obtain the following privileges, viz: 1—Right to establish a woollen mill and factory; 2—To get Danish and Norwegian farmers to go over to Iceland and there start experimental farms and teach the inhabitants how to cul-tivate and till the land; 3—To make experiments in tree planting; 4—To aid the fishermen and seamen to obtain better boats, nets, tackle and other requisites for the trade; 5—To teach them how to dry and salt the fish and to instruct them in salting mutton for ex-port.

King Frederick Fifth accepted the schedule, just as Skuli had presented it and ratified the regulations contained therein and the shareholders were so well satisfied with Skuli's success that they contributed the sum of 20,000 kroner, which equals in our money a little over five thousand dollars, with which to estbalish the woollen factory and mill and made arrangements with the people of Reykjavik, that if they allowed the factory to be started there, that town would become the capital of the kingdom.

Thus in the year 1752, by the building of the factory at Reykjavik, was the foundation of the present capital laid. It was about this time that the merchant company of Copenhagen rented the right of commerce in and with Iceland and it was well known that this company was noted for the practice of ustary and extortion. The Merchants' company were much annoyed, when they found that the woollen mills had been started, as it would break up the monopoly they had of the trade and commerce of the whole island and refused to transport any products of the factory in their vessels to foreign countries. So in order to protect this infant industry Skuli received permission to transport whatever the mill turned out to Copenhagen and sell it there.

Skuli had a bitter fight with the monopoly, i.e., the Merchant company, and it is with regret that we find that about this time several bad seasons came in succession, which naturally very much lessed the profits of the shareholders. But the king, knowing how matters stood, advanced them money to keep it going. None of the industries made any satisfactory progress except the woollen mill. In fact the famine was so severe in the land that many of the inhabitants starved. The Merchant company did not fulfil their contracts and agreements to supply the islanders with general merchandise and the whole country was in distress. Finally a law suit was instituted against the company and the government ordered the Merchants' company to relinquish their contract for the monopoly of the commerce of Iceland, in two months from the date of the command, which they did in the year 1758. Trade and commerce was again carried on under the king's orders for a few years and the people were greatly benefitted and more satisfied than when it was under a company's rule.

But the king found that it caused a lot of expenses and much extra work for the government and in the year of 1763 the debt of the Icelanders to the king for merchandise was the large sum of 258,924 rikisdalir (equal in our money to 129,462 dollars), so the king thought it better to again rent the business. So in the 1764 he accepted an offer from the Merchants' company agreeing to allow them the privilege of the output of the factory much against the wishes of Skuli, the governor.

As soon as the Merchants got hold of the right of the woollen mill, they did all in their power to starve out the industry and to benefit themselves by doing so. Skuli, however was putting forward every effort to save the factory from being shut down. He brought a lawsuit against the company, stating that the company had not complied with the agreement as arranged and ordered by the king and that they had in many cases brought over and sold to the people produce that was not fit for use. So the Danish government took the matter up and made them pay an indemnity of 4400 rikisdalir (equal to 2200 dollars.)

JonEirikson finally induced the Danish government to again take over the trade and commerce of Iceland, from the Merchants' company which it did in the year 1774 and it was continued on and for the account of the king until the year 1778.

The case which Skuli had brought against the Merchants' company, relative to the woollen factory was settled in favor of himself and the shareholders. But, he, seeing there was not any possibility of the shareholders ever making anything out of it and to save the factory from destruction relinquished his and their claims and gave it over to the government who ran it for a few years and then closed it, which was during the latter part of the century and it has never been run since.

However the benefit derived by its having been in operation, was that the people of the country learned how to prepare their wool for the market and this industry was very much improved.

Skuli Magnuson became quite an old man before he died, which was in the year 1794.

Eggert Olafson and Bjarni Palson.

During the latter part of the 18th century the king appointed two commissioners to inspect Iceland. One was Eggert Olafson and the other Bjarni Palson; both of these men were Icelanders, but were highly educated men having studied at the University of Denmark. Eggert was thoroughly versed in both philology and natural philosophy and Bjarni, as equally well educated in the science of medicine. They travelled all over Iceland from the year 1752 until 1757 and not only visited all the inhabited portion of the country, but a large part of that which is uninhabited. They collected quantities of herbs and natural curiosities and fossils and transported them to Copenhagen and there they received money from the government to provide a way in which to preserve the collection and write a work concerning their mission and observations while travelling in Iceland. Bjarni was, however, appointed as head physician to the island in the year 1760, he being the first physician to be appointed to this office before. He served in this capacity faithfully, well and energetically until his death, which took place in 1799. Eggert wrote a book which is one of the best books which has ever been written about Iceland. In the year 1766 he left Copenhagen for Iceland and resided with Bjarni Halldarson in Saudlaukdal, who was the head priest of the district and well known for his knowledge and experience in gardening, fruit culture and general knowledge of horticulture. Eggert was appointed a lawyer but unfortunately was drowned in Broad Bay, on the 30th of May, 1768, in the 41st year of his age.

Deep sorrow and regret was felt all over the country when the news of his death was announced. No one was better acquainted with the land or its productiveness, no one acquired a more intimate knowledge of its beauty and usefulness to the people, no one knew more than he the amount of prosperity that might be gained by

properly utilizing it.   He was the)est poet that ver wrote on the
)eaities of nature and farming.   He knew fill well the necessity
of the nation's cultivating the soil, to gain headway. He was never
known to complain of ill-luck, as the poet who preceded him used to,
but always tried to enliven the hearthstone and awake the ieople
from their lithargy to use their energies towards progression. In one
of his poems he describes the delight of a farier's life, and paints
in superb word-pictures the joys and charms of nature.

Eggert was a great logician and had siblie fantasies of the
futire of the country and told the people that aoove all things they
should endeavor to preserve the pirity of the Icelandic langtage, as
it was)ecoming degraded and de)ased)y admixture with foreign
words.   But the people were in sich a state of apathy and ignorance
that few took any heed of what he said.

Jon Eirikson and the Government of the Land and Financial Condition.

In the year 1770 the governor of Iceland was ordered to reside
on the island. The land being divided into two judicial districts, a
bailiff was appointed over each division.   The governor, however,
acted as)ailiff over the soith and west while the other)ailiff looked
after the north and cast; later on the west part was divided from the
soith and another)ailiff was appointed.

During the sale year a committee was appointed to inspect the
land and report on the condition.   This committee was appointed
by the king and consisted of three iei)ers who went over to Iceland and collected a vast a)oint of statistical and other inforiation
from the inhajitants.

The reason of their having)een sent to Iceland was that in the
year 1769, Pal Viddalin and Jon Eirikson pu)lished a book in the
Danish language a)out the progress of Iceland.

Jon Eirikson was a professor of law at the University of Soreyar
and highly honored for his learning.   He)egan his schooling in

Skalholt,)ut went to Denmark with Revd. Harboe, who asissted him in o)taining his University edication. In the year 1771, he was appointed to an office under the governmint of Icelandic legislation, and also did considera)le work in connection with)oth Danish and Norwegian affairs. Owing to his energy, intelligence, forethought and pleasant manners to everyone, he was two years later promoted and)eca ie one of the high officials connected with Icelandic affairs. From the year 1773 until the year 1787 the Danish government used more energetic measures and took a greater interest in Icelandic affairs than ever)efore or since. Jon Eirikson was full of patriotic enthusiasm for his native land and did his utmost to further the)etterment of Iceland's financial condition)y o)taining better regulations and having everything done he could, to help to increase the raising of produce and other industrial employments that would)e)eneficial to the Icelanders. He found it extremely hard to advance, at any)ut a slow rate, owing to the many difficulties that come up from time to time, for instance in the year 1761 hoping to i)prove the stock and quality of the sheep and wool.

They imported from Spain a new)reed,)ut unfortunately by the rascality of the traders, they were found to be infected with a disease called 'sca),' which spread at such a fearful rate over the whole of the flocks that it beca ie an epidemic and the people were una)le to combat the pest and only succeeded in checking it)y killing all the weak and suspected sheep, which were slaughtered by co i mand of the king and even after that the 'scab' destroyed many for some time.

In the year 1779 occurred one of the most appalling incidents in our history. This was the eruption of a volcano and was the most destructive that we have ever heard of in the history of our country, in fact since the first settling. This occurred in the eastern part of the island and)roke out in several places. It first was noticed in the summer of 1783 and lasted until the middle of the winter of the following year. The grass was compeletely destroyed; the atmosphere)ecame dense and full of nausious vapors,)eing like a heavy cloud all over the land the whole time and this has been called ever since 'The vaporous famine. In one year, 1783 to 1784, 11,-000 cows, 27,000 horses and 186,000 sheep died from its effects, or four-fifths of the entire number of sheep on the island, and naturally when the domestic animals starved and died, the people could subsist but a short time longer and consequently during the year 1784 and 1785 more than 9,000 of the people succumbed, most of them dying from starvation. In the south part of the island in 1784, an earthquake took place and many people thought the island would be altogether destroyed.

In 1785 a committee was appointed in Copenhagen to inspect and find out exactly the state of affairs and the circumstances the people were in and also to endeavor to find some means by which they could improve the condition of the people and it was decided to remove the bishop's headquarters and also the school to Reykjavik because nearly all the buildings had been destroyed in the earthquake.

The school was accordingly removed and the real estate sold. But the bishops, Finnur Jonson and Hannes Finnscn were by their own desire, allowed to remain there as long as they lived.

The committee discussed very seriously removing all the Icelanders to Denmark and decided to give the Danish merchants the commercial rights free.

In the year 1788 Jon Eirikson was one of the committee, but he had labored so hard, more especially with literary work, that it affected his health. He was the head librarian for the king, and had put the library into perfect order and conveniently arranged it. He was very much dissatisfied with the doings of the committee, of which he was a member, and strenuously opposed the moving of the seat of the bishop and the school from Skalholt to Reykjavik and protested against the selling of the real estate. He also endeavored to force the merchants to reside in Iceland, when they had received the free gift of the right of trade, but he was over-ruled and so the matter became law.

He being of a sentimental nature and naturally unhealthy, with these troubles and his feeling of despair at Iceland's condition and prospects, he succumbed on the 29th of March in the year 1787.

John Eirikson was a scientific man and wrote many essays. He was a noted author and during his life he succeeded in having established in Copenhagen an educational association, and from the year 1779 until his death he remained as president of it. The object of this association was by every possible means, to further education and induce the Icelanders to turn their thoughts in the right direction on educational matters and improve not only their minds and morals but also their physical development.

They printed a periodical review, of which fifteen volumes have been published.

General Petition.

After the committee appointed by the king had given the commercial rights free to the Danish merchants a committee was appointed to take charge of all the commercial property in Iceland, such as buildings and other things and chattels belonging to them and which were used for commercial purposes. This property was appraised and then sold and the Danish government assisted the Danish merchants to purchase them on easy terms, also aiding them with money to get commerce on a solid footing and in proper shape to enable them to supply the necessary produce and mercantile goods that were used and needed by the Icelanders.

But commerce was not improved because the merchants knowing that Iceland was a Danish dependency, endeavored to take as much money out of the people as they possibly could and the Icelanders themselves, through the Machiavelian practices of the monopoly had relapsed into apathy and indifference and almost total disregard for their welfare. The monopoly had put so many obstacles in the way, hindering all operations that may have been projected for the benefit of the people, as for instance, when the woollen factory and mill were started they obliged the people by refusing to supply them with necesaries, to abandon the project, thus forcing the people to buy of the monopoly, more than they otherwise would have done. Energy, will power and progress were at a very low ebb. Honor, straightforwardness and generosity almost unknown; the merchants holding the farmers in great contempt and then when opportunity offered cheated them as much as they could. Naturally this caused a great deal of dissatisfaction amongst the farmers and in consequence, thinking retaliation would help them, began to put up their produce and wares in a deceptive manner, thinking that in taking advantage this way they would get even, not noticing that at the same time they were working against their own interests at a later time. Thus the prices they received began getting lower and lower until at last they ceased to take any pains at all in preparing their produce, not putting it up or packing it uniformly. In fact business was stagnant and the people were losing all ideas of business probity and prosperity waned. The so-called 'free trade' was a decided failure and the best men of the country recognized that there must be more freedom in trade relations and this could only be done by competition if the islanders were to be benefited. In the year 1795 at Althing, to endeavor to help his compatriots Magnus Stevenson, a lawyer, circulated a petition which all the leaders signed, with the exception of the governer, asking the king to allow foreigners to enter Icelandic ports for the purpose of trade, admitting them free, thus allowing competition, which would no doubt have helped the islanders. They also accused the merchants for their extortion and cheating while trading with the people.

This petition was called 'The General Petition of Iceland.' But naturally the merchants worked hard against it. And as it was an easy matter for them to appear before the government and make up any kind of a story they wished, it was not very difficult for them to persuade the government that they had been misrepresented by the people of Iceland. This caused the king to reprimand all the officers who signed the petition, at the same time denying the people any commercial liberty.

Althing Abolished.   Superior Court of Justice.

During the 17th and 18th centuries Iceland was in a most de-plorable condition.   Almost every other year there was a famine, although the seasons were no worse than they had been that time or even before, but if there was an eruption or if the polar ice came oftener than usual the people were in such a lethargic state and so despairing that, instead of doing all they could, they were not able to protect themselves from starvation.   Can it be then wondered at, that in these centuries the king's power increased and that of Althing declined, until the 18th century when it sank into insignificance and finally ceased to use its legislative authority. In the year 1774 both the grand and petit juries dwindled down to nine altogether. They did not care to come to Althing from the north quarter, so the juries were taken from the nearest districts.

In the year 1798, Althing was held for the last time on 'Thing-vall' and there were only 12 men in attendance and they only stayed for a few hours.   The jury chamber was in a ruinous, condition and unfit for use.   The two years following Althing was held in Reyk-javik, where a small population of about 300 had gathered.   The ancient Althing had faded from the present era.   In the year 1800 Althing was annulled by order of the king and a superior court of justice established in Reykjavik, which consisted of three judges and one head man, this was Magnus Stephenson.   It was about this time that the schools both of Skalholt and Holum were removed from their respective sites and united at Reykjavik. The accom-modation for the students being insufficient, they removed it from there to Bessastad and by the year 1805 the school was in a flourish-ing condition, owing to the fact that the accommodations were better and the teachers more capable.

The bishopric of Holum was also abolished and all the property and real estate sold, one bishop being appointed to rule all the churches and he resided at Reykjavik, the bishop of Skalholt re-ceiving the office.

Magnus Stephenson and the Educational Association.

Magnus Stephenson, the chief justice of Iceland, established in 1794 an educational association for the purpose of increasing learning and knowledge amongst the people. He was the mainstay and life of the institution. He purchased the printing press and materials from 'Trappey and also that at Holum; these he removed to Leirargarda. He wished to improve literature, as he considered the education of the people was much behind the times and needed reformation, to bring it up to the manner or fashion in which it was used in other countries, in other words he wanted everything to be up to date. He printed pamphlets or small books which he called by the name of 'Remarkable News' and many good books. One remarkable specimen was the history of the 18th century which is considered the best in that class of history in Iceland. During the war between Denmark and England, he was unable to obtain any paper, so he had to give up printing until the war was over. As soon as he could, he again commenced and printed a monthly pamphlet which he called 'Cloister Posten. These he continued to publish for nine years, 1818—1825 and 1827. Magnus was notable for his great energy and learning. He repeatedly printed books, one following the other in quick succession, but he found that the people were too conservative and so education did not advance as rapidly as it might. The people as a rule did not seem to care for new books. Many of them understood his purpose, others were envious of his energy, others over his circumstances, some thought him domineering, thus showing their ingratitude.

For them he sacrificed his own benefit by publishing the very best books he could procure. He got into the habit of writing discussions and created a great deal of dissatisfaction amongst certain classes. He unfortunately was not well acquainted with Icelandic literature as he should have been and consequently was unable to publish anything suitable for the lower classes. He died in the year 1833 and the educational association ceased to exist.

The Hostility of Jorgenson.

During the years 1807 and 1814 hostilities continued between Denmark and England. But very few merchant vessels came to Iceland. This caused an immense amount of hardship and a great want of merchantile produce. The people also had a very hard struggle to get enough to eat even with what they could grow and raise themselves and were forced to use Iceland Moss, Dulse or edible seaweed and angelica roots for human food and Dyer weeds for dyeing and a few commenced to cultivate gardens. Horse-shoes and stirrups were made out of horns because no iron could be obtained.

Late in June, 1809, an English man-of-war arrived at Reykjavik and amongst the crew was an English merchant by the name of Phelps and a Dane by the name of Jorgen Jorgenson. They arrested the governor, Earl Trampe, and took him on board their ship. Jorgenson put up notices in Reykjavik, stating that the island was not under Danish jurisdiction any more and that Denmark had nothing whatever to do with it. He took all property belonging to any of the Danish merchants and all the king's money he could get his hands on. He promised the people to release them from paying any taxes to the king of Denmark or any debts they might owe the Danish merchants. The land was to receive full liberty; he promised many improvements and took the governing of the land into his own possession till the next year, when he said the government would be elected by the people. He called himself protectionist of Iceland and ruler of land and sea. The population of Reykjavik was about 750. They had no arms and the ship could easily have destroyed the town whenever the commander chose. The people however naturally thought that the English government had ordered him to act, so they acted carefully until they could get word from Denmark, although some wanted to fight with Jorgenson, but cooler and wiser heads saw it would not help them. In August another English man-of-war arrived. They arrested Jorgenson and took him to England. Magnus Stephenson took charge of the government until the king of Denmark should determine what course to pursue. Peace was proclaimed in 1810 and the king of England made a treaty with the king of Denmark that the Icelanders and England should trade together. But commerce was at a very low ebb and little was doing or had been done while hostilities were continuing and times were very hard in Iceland during that period.

Literature Introduced Again.

In the 19th century there began a new era in the literature of the century. The poetry was more of a romantic nature. This had a great effect on education, inculcating a deeper knowledge of history, philology and philosophy. The poets wrote of ancient times and the heroes of those periods. The great poet of Denmark, Ochlenschlager, by name, also took the subjects for his poems from the histories of the northern kingdoms and learned men turned their attention in their writings to the ancient poems and histories and they became more of a national character. They began to prove the origin of the nation, its life, its history and progression in education, compare the different languages and deeds of their fore- fathers and found valuable manuscripts written in the Icealndic language. Rasmus Christian Rask, a Dane, and one of the most erudite philologists, was impressed by the Icelandic language and stated that the Norwegian vernacular was the mother of the lang- uages of Northern Europe and that Icelandic was similar to Norwe- gian.

He went to Iceland for the purpose of learning and studying the language, and remained there from the year 1813 to 1815. He visited many places of interest while he was there and tried to estab- lish an educational association to keep the Icelandic language in its original purity. He discussed the matter with a priest named Arna Helgason and other leading men, but could come to no agreement so on his return to Copenhagen he obtained the co-operation of Bjarna Thorarinson and Finn Magnuson, both of whom were Ice- landers. Finn Magnuson was a scientific scholar. In the year 1816 the three men met and then formed the 'Icelandic Book Edu- cation Association,' of which there are two departments, one in Reykjavik, in Iceland, and the other in Copenhagen, in Norway and Rask made this association a national affair.

The Board of Directors had to be Icelanders or men thoroughly acquainted with the Icelandic language. The following year they published 'The Sturlung,' which instructed and gave interesting matter on the subject, there never having been anything of the kind published before. Later on 'Annals' were written by Police Magistrate Jon Espolin and a geography of the country published by Gunnlaug Oddson and others.

The Book Education Association commenced to reform educational affairs with good success and did all they could to fulfill the regulations that had originally been promulgated. They printed every year many works, which are remarkable and did and are doing more to increase and extend the education of the Icelanders and the honor of their nation in foreign countries, the board of directors always consisting of the most honorable and erudite men.

Bjarni Thorarinson.

With the poems of Bjarni Thorarinson begins the romantic Icelandic poetry, telling of doubty deeds and the romances of ancient times. He was quite a youth when he first attended the school of Copenhagen, when the movement spoken of above was but in its infancy. He was well versed in the history of his country, having been reared on that historical spot known as Hlidarenda, where Gunnar, the great hero, had lived and died and whose douty deeds and heroism are the pride of the nation. When Bjarni was residing in Copenhagen, he was never tired of speaking about its old heroes and was continually speaking in praise of their ability and intelligence. But alas! men are

BJARNI THORARINSON

not of the same stamina as they were then and we have to look al.

most in vain, to find men their equal at the present time. When Bjarni was 18 years old he wrote the song 'Eld gamla Isafold' which was made the national anthem and has continued as such to the present day. He has also written many other songs; was very patriotic and wished to put vim into and make improvements and advance in education among his fellow citizens.

With Bjarni's writings a new period was created in Icelandic lyric. He was a man of visionary ideas and humanity, but sad and serious in his poems. His funeral commemorative songs are considered the purest and best of lyrics of Iceland today.

The 6th Period, 1830—1874. Fighting For Liberty. Althing Again Established.

Up to this time the leading Icelanders only worked to increase their financial condition and improve the education of the people. They tried to induce the people to establish means of subsistance for themselves, to obtain liberty in trade and commerce and to teach the people profitable industries. But in 1830 they began to strive for the improvements of the political situation because liberalism was fast spreading all over Northern Europe. This was the cause of Frederick 6th creating two consulative assemblies, one for Jutland and the other for the islands, as they were then called, and Icelanders were attached to the island's consultative assembly, and the Danish government asked, the bailiffs of Iceland, in which way the proportional representation could be skilfully established so as to harmonize with the Danish.

Liberalism greatly affected the Icelandic students, who resided in Denmark. Baldvin Einarson was the leader. He was a true patriot and very energetic. He wished to awaken his countrymen to political progress and published a periodical by the name of 'Arman on Althing' in which he set forth the old glory, energy and progress of Iceland. He put in articles on the consultative assembly, both in

Icelandic and Danish. He wanted to have a consultative assembly for the Icelanders in Iceland on 'Thingvall' and all the Icelandic officials sided with him. But the governor was against it and finally concluded to send representatives to Denmark.

In the year 1837 Bjarni Thorarinson, a bailiff of the north east part, and Pall Nelsted, a police magistrate, got up a petition to the king to grant them a consultative assembly in Iceland.

But the king refused and ordered that 10 of the officials of Iceland should meet at Reykjavik and discuss all political matters there every other year.

In the year 1839 Christian the 8th became king of Denmark. He was a wise and good king and a kind friend to the Icelanders. All those who were in Copenhagen congratulated the new king and at the same time presented him with an address, praying him to grant that they might have a consultative assembly of their own ruled over by the best men of the land and administer their own affairs.

In the year following, 1840, the king ordered the committee of Icelandic officials, which met at Reykjavik as usual, to take into consideration as to whether it would be better or not to have a consultative assembly in Iceland and meet in the old place at Thingvall and call it 'Althing.' in remembrance of the good days of old.

All the most prominent Icelanders were at first somewhat suspicious of these proposed improvements in their affairs and seriously pondered over and discussed the question and finally on the 8th of March, 1843 they decided to establish 'Althing' and act as such at Reykjavik two years later.

Fjolner and Jonas Hallgrimson.

JONAS HALLGRIMSON.

In the year 1833 Baldvin Einarson died at the age of 31 years and two years later four young Icelanders clubbed together and published a periodical review in Copenhagen, under the name of 'Fjolner' their names were Brynjolfur Peturson, Jonas Hallgrimson, Konrad Gislason and Tomas Samundson. The latter, however, had gone to Iceland the year before as a priest. The object of this review was to endeavor to wake up the people and put some life into them. The Review was published for nine years in succession and was a masterly and well written work.

Thomas Samundson was the most progressive of the publishers and two years later was travelling abroad to learn the ways, manners, modes of doing work, and other interesting subjects for the benefit of the Review and also the nation. He was very patriotic and did all he could to not only improve the minds of the people and their industrial pursuits, but more especially in education. Although his health was failing he refused to give up this labor of love and continued writing to the last, in fact as long as he could hold a pen in his hand. He accomplished a large amount of work during his life time. He died at the age of 34 in the year 1841 and the same year saw the death of Bjarni Thorarinson.

Konrad Gislason wanted to reform the Icelandic language and wrote about it in 'Fjolner' (The Review). He studied the Icelandic grammar, upheld and corrected it and is considered to have been the best posted man in the Icelandic language that ever lived.

jonas Hallgrimson was a poet whose lyrical songs were so much admired and had great influence with people. He could draw brighter word pictures of the earth, sea and sky, the beauty of the fields, the song of the waterfall, the murmurings of the brooks, the soughing of the wind through the trees, the grandeur of the glaciers and the songs of the birds, in fact of all bright things, than any poet ever wrote before or since. He was a naturalist by profession and made a large collection of nature's curiosities. Many of his songs are the best we have in the country.

He died ten years after starting the Periodical Review.

Jon Sigurdson and Form of Government 1851.

JON SIGURDSON,

When King Christian 8th had ordered Althing to be established, the Icelanders in Copenhagen established a new periodical, the object of which was to give better articles about the establishment of the Althing and other matters of vital importance about the land, industrial and profitable enterprises which were to come in the future. Jon Sigurdson was the author of the work. He was 30 years of age, was a student in philology and Icelandic history, also he was thoroughly acquainted with all national matters. His knowledge was of more benefit to the country than that of any one else in Iceland and this fact caused him to reverence his native land and he spent his whole life working for its advancement and prosperity and cheerfully sacrificed his own interest for the furtherance of any political scheme which would be of benefit to the country and for this reason he was chosen to champion the cause of political liberty, for which he fought with energy, determination and patience to the last.

In the year 1848 liberalism was being fought for in the northern part of Europe with greater fervor and this naturally affected Iceland more or less. In that year good King Christian died and Frederick 7th became king of Denmark. He however soon after turned over the reins of government into the people's hands and the kingdom became a limited monarchy and many great changes were made in governmental affairs in Denmark and a special department formed for the government of Iceland and the prime minister was Brynjolfur Peterson, but to the regret of the Icelandic people, he did not live long after his appointment.

The following year a new constitution was established in Denmark and in Iceland the people also looked for a new constitution, and there was one to be sent, before it should become law, so that the Icelanders should have a voice in the matter and discuss it over amongst themselves. The Icelanders wished to have a government of their own which would meet in the island and have Althing legislative power.

In the year 1851 a mass meeting was called at Reykjavik to discuss the constitution for Iceland. But the conservatives were in power at the time in Denmark and they sent an army corps to Reykjavik to keep the peace. The inhabitants were surprised because no one had any thought of rebellion. The Danish government ordered Trampe, the governor, to put before the meeting a statement about the position of the island in the kingdom.

In Copenhagen the Danish government wished to have the same constitution in Iceland as was approved for Denmark, just as it was and without any comparison of the difference between the two countries in their wants and circumstances. This occurred on June 8th, 1849.

The constitution they wished passed read as follows. For the government of Iceland the legislative power should be in the hand of the king and that Althing only have power to act on smaller cases and all of the special ones should be called Danish cases. The Latin school, which had been removed to Reykjavik, was to be accounted as under Danish jurisdiction and the Danish treasury was to pay the expenses of the school. All the high officials in Iceland were to be paid by the Danish government as being Danish officials and to off-set that, all rent of real estate, all revenues from titles, or duty of any kind were to be paid into the Danish treasury. The Danish government were to make all regulations necessary for the government or revenue for the king. But the island should have all revenue from real estate belonging individually to the inhabitants and pay thereon to Althing for the salary of the lower officials and other men necessary for the enforcement of the laws, etc., i.e. those who did not receive pay from the Danish government.

The Danish government was to make all the principal laws for Iceland and Iceland should be entitled to representatives in Denmark, four for the House of Commons and two for the senate.

The Danish were not prepared to grant home rule to Iceland, but wished to govern it from Copenhagen as a province of Denmark, in the same manner as the Faroe islands. But this was entirely different from what the people of Iceland expected, according to the covenant King Christian 8th had promised, the Liberals of Denmark had agreed to, and as the people of Iceland had petitioned for, the meeting refused to accept the proposition as it was then laid before them by the Danish government, so they drew up a code of articles for conducting the affairs of Iceland for themselves.

By this code Iceland was to receive home rule, with the king as head regulator of political matter connected with the island and have the same king over them as ruled in Denmark, and that the king's title should be 'King' of Denmark, Iceland, etc., etc., and he should have the right to determine what cases or affairs in Iceland should be united to Danish jurisdiction. All matters, being the same in both countries, should be governed in Denmark, Iceland to take her part of it and pay the necessary expenses. According to or in portion to the amount of population or property in Iceland, also that Iceland should have a minister in the Danish government who would have a seat and vote, when matters concerning Iceland came before the house.

While the meeting was discussing the aforesaid measure or code the governor wanted to close the meeting at once. But Jon Sigurdson refused and all the rest of the people sided with him.

Commercial Monopoly Abolished.

The first half of the 19th century commercial monopoly held sway in the island. Even the best men in the country tried to have it abolished. Thomas Somundson and Jon Sigurdson wrote protestations against the monopoly, desiring commercial liberty and this awoke the apathy of the inhabitants at once. The Icelandic students were the first to take steps in Copenhagen. They demanded of Althing that they would look closely into the matter and do all in their power to obtain commercial liberty for the nation and many other petitions were sent from different quarters to Althing couched in the same terms.

The Danish merchants did all in their power to frustrate this movement they possibly could and said they were doing so for the benefit of Iceland, because they knew that if trade were opened up for all foreigners as well as themselves their profits would diminish and said that the Islanders would have to face starvation for want of necessary merchandise and produce.

When the hostilities ceased between Denmark and England the Danish merchants thought the commercial benefit derived by them from Iceland should not be taken away. But they did not care for the inhabitants of Iceland, who were paralized by the monopoly and handicapped as they were all thought of progress and energy were flagging. Some time later the Danish government sent a statement to the national meeting at Althing, regarding commercial liberty for Iceland. And Althing somewhat improved it but it did not make it as thorough as it should have done. The matter however was delayed by the Danish government and the Danish merchants used all the influence that could be brought to bear to defeat the measure.

But Senator Hirck and Balthazar Christenson forced the government to pass the measure. In the year 1857 the draft of com nercial laws was completed and approved, which allows any foreign nation to trade with Iceland in any harbor authorized for such purposes, this was of immense advantage to the islanders and trade grew rapidly, but the Icelanders did not advance very much in endeavoring to produce more for market. The Icelanders however were able to sell several articles; they could not before under the old regime dispose of such as horses and sheep and commerce was divided mostly between Scotland and England, which caused much competition between them and the Danes, and Iceland was consequently benefited. But even yet the law was deficient. It obliged the merchants to have representative members reside in the island and become actual residents. The same law applied to the Faroe Islands.

Unfortunately the Icelandic merchants did not exert themselves to bring business up to a proper standard and strive for progression and for this reason the business in the island is not what it ought to be or would have been if more enterprise could have been engendered; the British merchants who instead of trading, buy and sell for cash only.

The Faroe islands have abandoned the commercial law and all trade is transacted on a money basis. Since the commercial laws of 'free trade' was established no family, as far as is known, has suffered from starvation, although unfortunately the farmers later on had considerable trouble from the scab amongst their sheep, it having been brought over from England in 1856.

Finance and Constitution.

At the close of the national meeting, an account of which we have already given, the Danish government had done nothing towards improving the constitution of Iceland.

But in the year 1857 Althing sent a petition, asking the Danish government, to concede them executive power over their finances. But this was not paid much attention to, until the Danish House of

Commons had many times expressed the opinion that the laws relating to the financing of Iceland should be improved and that
Althing should control all revenue and duties belonging to and in
Iceland.   In other words have definite control over their own affairs.   For the reason that all taxes and revenue were at that time
paid into the Danish treasury and the salary of all Icelandic officials
paid by Denmark.   In the year 1847 the Latin school was removed
from Bassastad and enlarged.   And a school for the education of
those desiring to become clergymen founded at Reykjavik. At the ex-
poration of 10 years the expenses incurred were so much more than
the revenue, that the senate did not feel justified in paying out Danish money for the benefit of the Icelanders. So the king ordered a
committee of five to look into the finances of the country, three of
the members being Danes and two Icelanders, Jon Sigurdson being
one of those chosen.

The committee unanimously agreed that Icelandic financial
matters should be separated from those of Denmark and that a subsidy should be paid by Denmark yearly, as compensation for the real
estate that had been sold for the benefit of the Danish treasury. But
on other matters the committee was divided, on Sigurdson holding
that 250,000 kroner should be paid every year out of the Danish
treasury to Iceland, 100,000 kroner of it to be paid as an indemnity
for the amount received by the Danish government, for the sums
they received from the Merchants' company for the monopoly of
trade, which going as it did to enrich the Danish treasury, was not
fair to Iceland.   But the rest of the 250,000 was the actual price
the Icelandic real estate brought to the government of Denmark.
Jon Sigurdson also stated that Iceland should pay pro rata for the
up-keep of the king and his family, as the Danes were doing, and
that he presumed that with the addition of the necessary amount
thus incurred with the cost of such political suits that might have to
be decided on between the two governments, this would amount altogether to about 40,000 kroner a year.   The other members of the
committee, however, were not desirous of giving Iceland as large an
amount as 250,000 kr., but no order for what amount should be

paid, was agreed upon, and did not ask that Iceland should participate in the payment of money to the Privy-purse, that is, for the king's expenses.

In the year 1865 the Danish government sent a document relative to the separation of Icelandic financial affairs from that of Denmark and offered 84,000 kroner every year as a subsidy, for 12 years and at the expiration of that time they would determine what the yearly amount should be. The same document provides for the separation of the government of financial affairs, each country attending to its own.

But Jon Sigurdson refused to accept this statute and said that the Danish government never had legislative power over Iceland and could not conceive how it was possible they could expect the Icelanders to relinquish a law that never was in force. He with Althing demanded that the Danish government should pay a larger amount of subsidy and stated that they were ready to receive legislative powers to enable them to settle their own financial affairs. This declaration of their want occupied four paragraphs of the petition and Althing also renewed their demands for the formation of a new government under new dispensations. In the year 1867 Hilmar Finsen was governor of Iceland and the representative of the king and the government of Denmark, sent to Althing a statute, setting forth the form of government and rights of the Icelanders and stating that Iceland should have its own government and have jurisdiction over their own affairs, the executive powers of the legislature to rest with the king and Althing in conjunction with each other and the judges should rule all criminal and civil cases; that the king should appoint a minister who should reside in the island and be the head of its government and that the Icelanders should have the same political freedom as the Danes; that Althing should meet every third year in Reykjavik. These statutes were the most liberal of all that had been before offered by the Danish government (and in some of its ordinances was more perfect and preferable to the constitution of 1874. Althing approved these statutes in the main, but they demanded that the minister should be responsible to the government and Al-

MICROCOPY RESOLUTION TEST CHART

(ANSI and ISO TEST CHART No. 2)

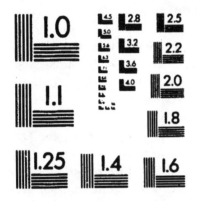

APPLIED IMAGE Inc

1653 East Main Street
Rochester, New York   14609   USA
(716) 482 - 0300 - Phone
(716) 288 - 5989 - Fax

thing for his acts, and that they could bring accusation against him, if necessary, before the chief court of justice; also that Althing should sit every other year and be divided into two legislative bodies. Althing also demanded 120,000 kr. subsidy yearly in place of the 100,000 offered. The Danish government placed the matter before the senate the following year, and Nelliman, a Danish minister, showed clearly the relative position of Iceland to the Danish rule and its privileges and reproved the government for making any modification concerning the financial affairs of Iceland. This dissention on his part stopped the progress of the establishment of home rule in Iceland, the Danish government thinking that Hilmar Finnson was asking too great a favor for his countrymen and prorogued Althing in 1869. After the new election for Althing in Iceland was over, the Danish government sent two separate statutes, one relative to the position Iceland held in the kingdom and the other regarding the form of government of the island. But these statutes did not give the islanders as much satisfaction nor did they grant as many privileges in some paragraphs in them as that of 1867, the majority of Althing demanding that the statutes should include all laws and regulations regarding the rule of the country. They also agreed to request the king not to make these statutes the laws to govern the island by, asking that another set of statutes should be given which would be as beneficial to Iceland as those of 1867.

But finally Althing agreed to approve the bill of constitution with some amendments and sent a petition that with these amendments it be made the law. The Danish government and Althing were no nearer a thorough amicable settlement than before. But to be rid of the matter and get it out of their hands they made the statutes and their amendments a law, showing the rights of Iceland in the kingdom on the 2nd of January, 1871.

This act of the Danish government, however, caused considerable dissatisfaction in the Island, on account of the fact, that it was not the same as the one partly accepted by Althing, the majority refusing to recognize these regulations as they kept out the necessary rules for the proper government of the island, at the same time they agreed that they should be respected as a declaration from the Danish government. A. F. Krieger, a remarkably learned man, and the Danish minister, who drew up the statutes said that they were perfectly complete. However, Althing with a few amendments to it, passed the bill.

Iceland is the only portion of the Danish kingdom that has special land privileges. It takes no part in the legislative power of the kingdom and sends no representatives to the Danish parliament for the sovereign and does not have to pay towards its support.

The special statutes connected with Icelandic rights are:—

1—Civic rights and jurisdiction of all penal and civil laws except supreme court cases.

2—Police control.

3—Supervision and right to make laws regarding churches and schools.

4—Regulating rules for the practice of medicine, doctors and sanitary conditions.

5—All poor laws.

6—Keeping up and opening of new roads and postal service.

7—Receiving all revenue derived from the island.

8—Up-keep of national property, public buildings and the treasury.

The subsidy was fixed at 60,000 kronur yearly and for ten years 40,000 for expenses, from which sum 2,000 kr. were deducted after the first payment every year for ten years, until nothing was left of the original sum.

The Danish government also agreed to pay all expenses of Icelandic high officials residing in Copenhagen, to subsidize the mail steamers between Iceland and Copenhagen and any accounts outstanding against Iceland were considered settled in full. In any light the matter could be looked at, this constitution was a movement towards progression in the government of Iceland.

In 1873 an earl was ordered over to Iceland to take the place of the governor which office was abolished. But he had no more power than the governor had before him as he was head of all officials of Iceland, and the Icelanders did not like this act of the Danish government as it was done without the knowledge or consent of Althing.

In 1873 the Danish government did not issue any statutes so that Althing might form a government, which caused much dissatisfaction amongst the people and they summoned a meeting on Thingvall and debated the matter. They issued petitions to Althing to take the matter into consideration, to attend to it very carefully and come to some definite conclusion if possible.

After deliberation Althing approved of a form of government for Iceland the same summer and took a step farther in demanding Home Rule, but wanted an earl and ministers for Iceland.

But Althing understood that the king would not ratify the form of government drawn up by it and they sent an earnest petition asking the king to grant 'Home Rule' in Iceland the next year and approve the form of government as drawn up by Althing as near as possible and some special matter they wished for. Attention was called particularly to, and the king issued, a constitutional law for Iceland in January, 1874. This marked a grand era in the history of Iceland, being the one thousandth year since the first Norwegian man settled there and the inhabitants were desirous of having a great universal festival all over the island.

King Christian 9th and the National Festival.

CHRISTIAN IX.

At the time above mentioned, King Christian 9th was king of Denmark. He came to the throne in 1863 and at a very critical period of the history of the nation, as Germany wished to annex the provinces of Lauenborg, Holsstein and Sleswic, which she accomplished by conquering the provinces one year later. By these means the king of Denmark lost more than one third of his subjects, and saw with sorrow how short sighted his ministers had been and how the result of his loss was liable to affect the future of Icelandic affairs. This occurred a long time after the monarchy was abolished.

In 1874 the national festival was celebrated and all Iceland was out in holiday array, to celebrate this great event in the era of the island, it being the one thousandth anniversary of the first settlement of Iceland and the inhabitants wished to make it the most notable of " festivals ever held. King Christian came to Iceland and the people received him cordially and he was pleasant to every one. He attended the celebration at 'Thingvall' and that at Reykjavik. The second of August was the galaday of the festival and holy masses were said over the whole land. But it was on the day before that the form of government or constitution was given by him to the people and came into force that day.

On leaving the island the king gave the sum of 10,000 kr. to create a fund for the benefit of industrial farming.

The Constitutional Laws.

These laws were the result of the outcome of the political feuds which had existed from the year 1848 till the day when the king gave the constitution on August 1st, 1874, which were a great improvement in the laws of the country, that had hitherto been in force, although they did not get as much 'Home Rule' as they had hoped for through Jon Sigurdson and Althing.

The Legislative power and financial affairs of the island were in the hands of Althing and it was divided into two bodies, the number of representatives being increased to 12 in the Upper House, (six of them being appointed by the king) and 24 in the House of Commons.

The executive power was partly dispensed by the Danish government and the Earl of the island received power to settle all cases, which otherwise had been taken to Copenhagen for jurisdiction and all statistics which formerly went to Copenhagen were sent to him instead. But the chief power was given to one of the Danish ministers of justice. This weakened the authority of Althing as the real executive power was under Danish influences.

But the minister in Denmark did not trouble the Earl, who was the originator of various measures issued to Althing, which became laws afterwards and very little interference was made with the workings of the Althing, the people taking care of their own affairs without any trouble from the Danish government.

The Legislative Assembly From 1874.

As soon as Althing had received the legislative power it commenced to aid many enterprises necessary to improve the situation mentally, morally and physically and the first thing that was done on the 1st July, 1875, was to approve of a salary for Jon Sigurdson, who although holding no office, had labored faithfully and hard for the political liberty of his nation, which he valued far above the emoluments of a governmental position. He was a member of the two first legislative assemblies, but owing to his health having broken down he could not attend the third and died on 7th December, 1879 at the age of 68.

The First Legislative Assembly Approved.

The first financial regulations for Iceland for the years 1876 and 1877, were approved by the Legislative Assembly, also laws regarding the medical profession, (the number of medical men was increased to 20) they also passed an act establishing a medical school at Reykjavik, and since that time the number of doctors has increased to 40, which was very necessary as the north part of the island was without physicians or any medical aid whatsoever, and passed many other laws necessary for the government of the island.

The acts relating to revenue have been improved; communication both by land and sea have been considerably increased and communication with other countries has greatly helped to increase the trade. Bridges have been built across the rivers and many new roads made and middle class schools and seamen's schools and four experimenal farms for teaching the newest and best methods of farming, also three schools for females and others have been subsidized, a national bank established in 1885 and in 1885 a general and charitable fund.

Inspection of the Constitution and Home Rule.

The great fault with the constitution was the controlling power of the Danish government. But the islanders' condition was greatly improved and progress was making fast strides for the advancement of the nation. But the two governments did not work in harmony as well as had been expected, because on many occasions Icelandic matter of importance, were delayed and the Minister of Justice at Copenhagen, on some occasions, had advised the king to veto laws that had been passed by Althing, which caused a feeling of dissatisfaction, for the king had on 23 occasions refused to sanction laws, which Althing had approved. They looked into the constitution and approved a new code of statutes at Althing in 1885, in which it was set for that they desired to have a Prime Minister appointed over the land, with ministers who should be Icelanders and reside in Reykjavik; they should be responsible for the government, the Prime Minister to Act as bailiff from the king and the ministers in Copenhagen to give up their positions and all offices there to be abolished.

In 1885 the Danish government sent a written notice to Althing in the name of the king, stating that Althing must not waste time and money in discussing the new code as it would not be accepted. But election to the Althing in 1886 was held and the constitutional code was approved, without any amendments. But the king refused to ratify it. At the next Althing the same discussions continued but nothing was done to decide the matter. In 1893 Althing again approved of the code of 1885 and the following year, after a new election, Althing again approved of the same measure. But again the king refused to ratify it.

In 1896 Althing tried to make an agreement with the Danish government to pay a special minister for the island. He was to be an Icelander and reside in the country and be responsible for his actions to the king and Althing and attend Althing whenever it met.

By this means they hoped to be able to have the entire management of their affairs. But the minister of Iceland, who was also minister of justice to the Danish government declined to accept this proposition. He had been twenty years in the office but went out in 1896. He had made some amendments to the constitutional bill which was issued on Althing in 1897 and by these means he hoped to draw political power from Iceland to the Danish government. But the amendments were refused by Althing altogether.

When monarchy was abolished in Denmark the Conservatives came into power and ruled until 1891 in which year the Liberals again got possession of the reins of government, and believing in the tenets of liberalism, respected individual rights and self-government in Iceland, they agreed that Icelanders were best acquainted with and had more intimate knowledge of their own affairs and would use their knowledge and do their best to improve their political and financial condition.

Albert who was minister of justice at that time in 1902 issued a code of constitutional amendments to Althing and the following acts and laws were contained in it: -

That a minister should be appointed for Iceland, who should be a native of that country.

That he should reside at Reykjavik.

That the Icelanders should pay his salary.

That he should be responsible for all executive actions to the king and Althing.

That he should abdicate his office for circumstances warranted by his actions in Iceland, but not in Denmark.

These amendments were approved on Althing in 1902 and again in 1903, October 3rd, these amendments to the old constitution were ratified by the king and early in the year 1904 a minister will be appointed to Iceland, and the office of minister to Iceland at Copenhagen abolished and replaced by one to be established at Reykjavik, consisting of the Prime Minister and his ministers and then the act of Home Rule for Iceland will have been consummated.

Progress and the Outlook.

In the last few years Icelandic farmers have been induced to improve their farms and by funds supplied by the 'Home Rule' government have been aided in doing so, they are beginning to understand commercial matters better and the necessity of being particular with their produce, so as to obtain the highest price for what they raise. They are establishing small creameries throughout the farming country, for the purpose of obtaining a better price for their butter. Our countrymen are far behind other nations in farming and other employments also in cleanliness in the preparation of the produce and other matters which have been a hindrance to progression and prosperity.

They have been too callou- of their interests, but the Merchants company's monopoly sapped the will power and energy of the nation, and the Danish government was inactive and negligent, taking no pains for the welfare of Iceland. It will take some years before the inhabitants will be able to become a thorough practical and business-like nation.

It is very necessary that the land should be cultivated before it can be of much benefit to the people. The old condition of things must be entirely eradicated and new methods of farming and the latest improvements in machinery adopted. Then in future years when the country is cultivated our dwellings rebuilt and up to date, sanitary matters attended to and everything about the homes made comfortable and in modern style, matters will be in a very different form from what they are at present.

The Icelanders are a very small nation and will have to use all the energy possible and strive keenly if they wish to progress morally, mentally and physically in keeping with the times.

The boys and girls who are willing to work for the benefit of their country must be energetic and strive to promote health, happiness, rectitude and all things beneficial to the interest of the country. To help one another and be charitable and bear with fortitude our trials, then their record will be handed down on the pages of their trials, then their record will be handed down on the pages of our history as an example worthy of imitation.

THE END.

TRADE AND COMMERCE OF ICELAND.

YEARS.	Import in 1,000 kr.	Export in 1,000 kr.	Import and Export in 1,000 kr.	The population.	Amount for each man.	
					Imports kr.	Exports kr.
1881-85..	6,109	5,554	11,663	71,225	85.8	78.0
1886-90...	4,927	4,153	9,080	70,260	70.2	59.2
1891-95...	6,415	6,153	12,568	71,531	89.7	86.2
1896...	8,289	7,527	15,816	75,854	109.3	99.2
1897......	8,284	6,590	14,874	75,663	109.7	87.1
1898... ..	7,354	6,612	13,966	76,237	96.6	86.7
1899... ..	8,253	7,851	16,104	76,383	108.1	102 8
1900... ..	9,276	9,512	18,783	76,303	121.5	124.7
1901......	10,522	9,691	20,213	78,470	134 1	123.7
1902.... .	10,854	10,602	22,456	79,428	136.7	133.5
1903... ..	12,068	11,292	23,360	79,800	151.1	141.6

The Capital of Iceland, Reykjavik, population, 8,000
Their Trade and Commerce in 1903. 5,889,640 kr.

The chief export from Iceland in the year—
Salted and dried fish, mostly cod..tons   15,000
Whale oil................. ....barrels   68,000
Cod liver and Seal oil .... ,,   12,000
Wool ....tons   800
Sheep ....number   15,108
Horses .... ,,   1,823

Their fishing fleet numbers 137 ships...tons 6,505.35
Their fishing boats number   1,906
Horses... ......   ,,   46 475
Sheep ....   ,,   696,680
Cattle .. . .   ,,   26,539
The value of 15 kroners is $4.

NOTE—For the benefit of my readers I have taken the liberty of adding to this work the above Statistical Tables which will give them an idea of the commerce of Iceland, both export and import, and also the population of our country. I have also given in a tabulated form the principal events and literary progress of the nation, which I trust they will find instructive.

Yours truly,

J. G. PALMASON.

The History of Iceland may be divided into the following periods.

THE COMMONWEALTH—400 Years.

THE HEROIC AGE.—850—1030 A.D.

	Literature, etc.	*Events.*
870—930 A.D.	Poetry of Western Islands.	Settlement by colonists from Norway, Ireland and Scotland.
930—980	Early Icelandic poets chiefly abroad.	Constitution worked out. Events of the early sagas take place.
980—1030	Icelandic poets.	Christianity comes in. Events of later sagas take place.

THE SAGA OR LITERARY AGE.

1030—1284	First era phonetic change.	Peace. Ecclesiastical organization.

LITERARY AGE.

1100—1150	Ari and his school—Thorodd.	Vernacular writing begins.
1150—1220	Saga writers. 2nd generation of Historians.	First Civil War 1208—1222. Rise of Sturlungs.
1220—1248	Snorri and his school. Biographers.	Second Civil War 1226—1258. Fall of great heroes.
1248—1284	Sturla. Second era of phonetic change.	Change of law 1271. Submission to Norwegian Kings.